Norfolk, Virginia

Registry of Free Negroes

1835–1861

ABSTRACTS

Compiled and Edited by
C. Bernard Ruffin

HERITAGE BOOKS
2014

HERITAGE BOOKS
AN IMPRINT OF HERITAGE BOOKS, INC.

Books, CDs, and more—Worldwide

For our listing of thousands of titles see our website
at
www.HeritageBooks.com

Published 2014 by
HERITAGE BOOKS, INC.
Publishing Division
5810 Ruatan Street
Berwyn Heights, Md. 20740

International Standard Book Numbers
Paperbound: 978-0-7884-5014-3
Clothbound: 978-0-7884-8432-2

The "registers" of free Negroes maintained in the Commonwealth of Virginia for nearly seven decades before the Civil War are an extremely valuable source of information for historians and genealogist.

In 1793 the Virginia General Assembly, concerned that large numbers of people of color were hiring themselves out, claiming to be free when in fact they were slaves, passed a law "to restrain the practice of negroes going at large." All free Negroes and Mulattoes were required to register with the clerk of the court where they lived—once a year, if they lived in one of the Commonwealth's independent cities (such as Richmond, Norfolk, Charlottesville) and every three years if they lived in a county (such as Fairfax, James City, or Isle of Wight).

After the enactment of the 1793 law, people who allowed their slaves to hire themselves out could be indicted by a grand jury while the offending slave languished in prison until his owner paid the jail fees. If a free person of color was unable to present his (or her) "register" to the authorities upon demand, he was subject to imprisonment as a runaway slave.

In 1806 the General Assembly passed another law that required that slaves emancipated after May 1, 1806 had to leave Virginia within twelve months or forfeit their right to freedom and be subject to sale by the Overseers of the Poor. In 1831, after the Nat Turner Rebellion, the law was changed so that free Negroes, liberated after 1806, who overstayed their welcome in the Commonwealth, could be sold at auction by the local sheriff.

In addition, the clerk notes the height of the registrant and any distinguishing marks or scars. Occasionally, other physical features, such as eye color, hair texture, and lip size are noted.

Fourth (#3), the clerk was required to explain the manner of manumission. Was the registrant born free? If not, was he (or she) liberated by means of a will or by a deed, and by whom?

Fifth (#4), the registrar recorded date or dates of registration. By the letter of the 1793 law, every free Negro should have registered every year, but this was not the case. Most people seem to have registered once (if, in fact, they registered at all). Some renewed their registration once or twice, often as a result of losing their papers. During the 1850s, the Norfolk city fathers seemed to have ordered a number of re-registrations. A great many people of color came from the outlying counties to Norfolk City "to labour therein." They were supposed to obtain a new registration immediately, but it seems that often the register from their old domicile was deemed sufficient.

Not all free people of color obtained a register. Since registration was intended primarily to distinguish free people from slaves in the work force, persons too old or too young to work frequently went unregistered.

Sixth (#5), 99% of the registers bear a date with the notation "ordered to be registered."Some freedom papers were "ordered to be registered" on the same date as their owner was registered, but, in most cases, this order came several years after the date of registration. Most likely, the city of Norfolk kept a record of free people of color in bound volumes which, over the years, were lost or destroyed. Indeed, some of the registers have a number in reference to a particular volume. It seems likely that once every few years, the court ordered that the copies of registration which were filed among the law causes be copied into these books.

The registers that exist for the city of Norfolk were prepared between 1835 and 1861, the first year of the Civil War, and record vital information for approximately 600 men, women, and children. Although the law of 1793 seems to have been enforced loosely, it is highly unlikely that it was completely ignored for forty years. It seems probable that for the first four decades after the passage of the law, copies of the registers were not retained after the information was copied into the now-lost books.

There is a seventh category (#6) for any other pertinent information on the register. On many of those from the 1850s the clerk stated whether or not the registrant was liberated before or after May 1, 1806. In some cases, he conceded that he did not know.

Using the indices to the U.S. Census provided by Ancestry.com as well as the Death Registers maintained by the City of Norfolk between 1853 and 1897, I have tried to find out what happened to the registrants. At least half appear not to be recorded in any subsequent census. If the man or woman was registered before 1850, when the U.S. Census first attempted to record the names of all free persons, there is the possibility that the individual died in the intervening years or, if she were a female, she married and took another surname. It seems, however, that nineteenth century census-takers missed a considerable percentage of the population.

There is a section, at the end of this volume, that includes thirteen free people who were hauled into court in the early 1830s, for failing to leave the state within twelve months of their emancipation. It appears that only in the year or so after the Nat Turner Rebellion in Southampton County did the officials in Norfolk attempt to enforce the 1806 law that ordered newly freed people of color to leave Virginia. Occasionally, in the late 1850s, the clerk noted whether or not permission had been granted the registrant to remain in the Commonwealth, but there is no evidence of any action taken against those who were lacking such authorization. Even in the case of the handful of people summoned to court, the notation "*Nolle presequi*" seems to indicate that the charges were dropped.

The Borough of Norfolk became the City of Norfolk in 1845, and was to be distinguished from Norfolk County, parts of which were annexed by the city in the nineteenth and early twentieth century, and which ceased to exist in 1963 when the remainder became the City of Chesapeake. Any reference to "Norfolk" is to the Borough/City; the county is identified as such.

ACHILLE, JAMES
(His register is partially crumbled and partly illegible)

1. Born circa 1815?
2. Height: 5'6", scarred by smallpox
3. Born free in Norfolk
4. Norfolk, [   ] 1852
5. August 23, 1858

_____, **ADELE** [Surname not given]
(Daughter of Sally)

1. Born circa 1816
2. Height: 4'10¼"; "Negro woman" of "light black complexion" with "two scars on left arm, below elbow joint and one near the wrist joint"
3. Emancipated by will of Ursula [Sautigan?], November 22, 1837
4. Norfolk, December 14, 1844
5. July, 1853

ALLEN, ANNE ELIZABETH

1. Born circa 1832
2. Height: 4'11"; "Small mark near left corner of left eye"
3. Born free in Norfolk, "the descendant of a female negro emancipated in this city since the first day of May, 1806.", "being proved by James Cheney"
4. Norfolk, October 29, 1851
5. 1853

AMES, PEGGY

1. "Born December 9, 1821"
2. Height: 5'9 or 10"; "Bright mulatto, round mark, about the size of a half dime, on back of left hand and underneath fingers, just below the lowest joint, large black mole on right arm, just below top of shoulder, scar from burn on back of neck and on top of right shoulder blade, other moles on and about back of neck"
3. Born free
4. Northampton County, October 9, 1848
5. October 22, 1849
6. Peggy Ames was enumerated by the U.S. Census on August 30, 1850 in Northampton County, one of three people of color in the household of the farmer Shepherd Ames. Peggy was described as 26 years old, "black", literate, and a native of Northampton County. No occupation was listed. Living with her was sixteen year old Mahaly Ames, 16 and "black."

ANDERSON, ANNA MARIA
("Child of Maria Anderson, a free mulatto woman")

1. Born circa 1825
2. Height: 5'1"; "Very bright mulatto complexion, with straight hair; no apparent mark or scar on head, face, hands."
3. Born free in Norfolk
4. Norfolk, April 23, 1838
5. July 25, 1853

ANDERSON, DEMPSEY

1. Born circa 1804
2. Height: 5'6"; "Mulatto with scar on right thumb from a cut"
3. Born free in Norfolk County, "removed therefrom to this city to labor therein"
4. Norfolk County, June 19, 1839; Norfolk, April 24, 1850
5. April 22, 1850 and July 26, 1858
6. Dempsey Anderson appears in the U.S. Census of the city of Norfolk in 1850. He is described as 46, mulatto, illiterate, and a house carpenter. Living with him is Marinda Anderson, black, 46 (evidently his wife), and Letitia Anderson, black, 66 (evidently his mother).

ANDERSON, ELEANOR

1. Born circa 1824
2. Height: 5'2½"; "Mulatto woman"
3. Born free
4. Gloucester County, September 7, 1846
5. July 26, 1858
6. "Permission is granted to Eleanor Anderson to go at large until next court, July 19, 1858, Wm. W. Lamb, Mayor" (July, 1858)

ANDERSON, LETITIA
(Daughter of Mary Ann Anderson, deceased)

1. Born circa 1839

2. Height: 5'¼" [she was 13]; "free girl of bright mulatto complexion" with "small scar on the side of neck"
3. Born free in Norfolk, proved by oath of William Robertson
4. Norfolk September 3, 1852
5. July 26, 1858
6. "Letitia Anderson is allowed to go at large till the next Court, Wm. W. Lamb, Mayor, July 20, 1858"
Miss Anderson was enumerated by the census in Norfolk in August, 1850 in the following household:
Mary A. Anderson, female, mulatto, 36
Ann M. Anderson, female, mulatto, 16
Mary E. Anderson, female, mulatto, 13
Letitia Anderson, female, mulatto, 11
Letitia Anderson, female, mulatto, 60
The older Letitia must have been the grandmother of Ann, Mary, and Letitia. The mother, Mary, must have died between August, 1850 and September, 1852.

ANDERSON, MARY ELIZA
("Daughter of Mary Anderson")

1. Born circa 1826
2. Height: 4'6" [she was 12]; Mulatto with "no apparent mark or scar on head, face, or hands; grey eyes and straight hair"
3. Born free in Norfolk, "on proved oath of Mary Sweney"
4. Norfolk, April 23, 1838
5. July 25, 1853

ANDERSON, WILLIAM

1. Born circa 1815
2. Height: 5'4"; "Scar on his nose between eyes and two small moles on left side of face, near mouth"
3. Born free in Norfolk County
4. Norfolk, July 28, 1838
5. July 26, 1853

_____ANDREW [No surname given]

1. Born circa 1821
2. Height: 5'10½"; "A light complected negro man with a small scar on the back of left hand."
3. Emancipated by will of George R. Corprew, "freedom fully established" April 6, 1846
4. Princess Anne County, November 1, 1847
5. January 24, 1848

_____, ANTHONY [No surname given]
See Wilson, Anthony

ARCHER, ELIZABETH

1. Born circa 1826
2. Height: 5'5"; "Negro woman of black complexion" with "scar on right arm near elbow, two small scars on back of right hand" [1850]; "Negro woman of black complexion" with "scar in the right arm, near elbow" [1855]
3. Born free in Norfolk, proved by oath of Elizabeth Thorpe
4. Norfolk, February 25, 1850 and April 30, 1855
5. March 26, 1855 and January 28, 1861
6. "I am unable to determine whether or not she is the descendant of a female negro emancipated since the first of May 1806" [1855]

ARCHER, SARAH

1. Born circa 1797
2. Height : 5'1", "Woman of light complexion...with a scar on her left arm and two marks on her breast."
3. Born free
4. Norfolk County, June 16, 1834
5. August 22, 1842

ARMISTEAD, CAROLINE
("Daughter of Nancy Ross, alias Nancy Sharp")

1. Born circa 1823
2. Height: 5'3" [at 16, in 1839]; 5'3¼" [at 33 in 1856] "Free negro girl of black complexion, no apparent mark or scar on head, face, or hands."
3. Born free in Norfolk
4. Norfolk, November 3, 1839, April 18, 1842, and May 29, 1856
5. August 26, 1851 and September 23, 1861
6. "Descendant of free negro born before 1st day May 1806" [1856]
   Enclosed in Armistead's freedom papers is the following note: "City of Norfolk. Caroline Armistead, a free woman, duly registered in the clerk's office of this court, and th captain of the steamer "Curtis Peck" will be justified in taking her from this city to Richmond. She is a woman of black complexion, thirty years of age, about five feet six inches high. Given under my hand at the city aforesaid this 4th day of June, 1855."

ARMISTEAD, GEORGIANNA
("Daughter of Nancy Ross a free woman")

1. Born circa 1829
2. Height: 5'3¼ ; "Negro girl of black complexion" with "scar on thumb of left hand"
3. Born free in Norfolk
4. Norfolk, January 2, 1839; [date torn off] 1849
5. May 22, 1854

ARTIST, DENNIS

1. Born circa 1819
2. Height: 5'10½"; "Black man [with] scar on forehead and one on chin and one over right eye."
3. Born free in Southampton County
4. Southampton County, October 15, 1849
5. October 15, 1849

ASHBY, JOHN

1. Born circa 1827
2. Height: 5'8¼"; "High mulatto, fair, smooth skin, no scar worth notice."
3. Born of free parents in York County
4. York County, July 17, 1848
5. April 23, 1849

AUSTIN, EDWARD
(Son of Tamer Austin)

1. Born circa 1833
2. Height: 5'3¼" [at 17]; "Negro boy of mulatto complexion" with "scar over left eye in eyebrow, scar on forefinger of right hand and scar on wrist of left arm"
3. Born free in Norfolk, proved by oath of Margaret D. [Casefeard?]
4. Norfolk, March 27, 1850
5. July 26, 1853
6. The census of Norfolk City on August 13, 1850 revealed:
   Joseph F. Allyn, 55, male, white, no occupation given, real estate valued at $32,000.00, born Massachusetts
   Elizabeth Allyn, 47, female, white, born Massachusetts
   William I. Moore, 30, male, physician, real estate valued at $1000.00, born Virginia
   Camilla Moore, 24, female, white, born Virginia
   Elizabeth Moore, five months, female, white, born Virginia
   Joseph F. Allyn, Jr., 10, male, white, born Virginia
   Edward Austin, 18, male, mulatto, born Virginia, cartman
   Anthony Poldore, 15, male, mulatto, born Virginia, ostler
   John Poldore, 15, male, mulatto, born Virginia, "none"
Austin must have been a servant within the wealthy household of Allyn, Sr. William Moore may have been Allyn's stepson.

AUSTIN, FANNY
(Daughter of Kizzy Austin)

1. Born circa 1828
2. Height: 4'10¼" [1843] 4'10 and seven eighths" [1853]; "free

negro girl of black complexion" with "scar on right arm near elbow and one on first joint of the right forefinger" [1843]. In 1853 the description was the same, except that she was a "woman", not a "girl" of "black complexion."

3. Born free in Norfolk, proved by oath of Margaret E. Casen
4. Norfolk, September 19, 1843 and August 27,1853
5. July 25, 1853 and August 27, 1858
6. Fanny Austin appears in the U.S. Census of 1850, living alone in Norfolk City. Her age is given as "26", her color as "black." She was illiterate, and no occupation was listed.

AUSTIN, JOHNSON
(Son of Kizzy Austin)

1. Born circa 1818
2. Height: 5'4"; "negro boy of black complexion with no apparent mark or scar on face or hands"
3. Born free in Princess Anne County
4. Norfolk Borough, March 29, 1837
5. August 26, 1851

BAKER, CATHARINE

1. Born circa 1830
2. Height: 5'4½"; "Negro woman of brown complexion [with] scar on her neck
3. Born free in Isle of Wight County
4. Isle of Wight County, October 2, 1848
5. February 25, 1850

BAKER, SUSAN MARTHA ANN ["Susan, alias "Susan Martha Ann Baker"]

1. Born circa1827
2. Height: 4"11¼" [1848]; 4'11½" [1849]; "Dark complexion, full face, bushy hair, scar on forehead between eyes" [1848]; "negro woman of dark complexion" with "scar on forehead, between eyes" [1849]
3. Born free in Surry County, by certificate of Doila [?] N. Stewart,

"having removed therefrom to this city to labour therein"
4. Surry County, January 22, 1848; Norfolk, December 31, 1849
5. December 29, 1849 and July 27, 1858
6. "Allowed to apply to next court, Wm W Lamb, Mayor, July 21, 1858"
"Daughter of Isabel, free woman"
"Martha A. Baker" was enumerated in the U.S. Census of 1850 for the City of Norfolk. She was described as age 20, "black", illiterate, with no occupation listed. She was living with Kitty Bird, 58 years old and "black", and also with no listed occupation.

BAKER, ZEDEKIAH

1. Born circa 1807 [1831] or 1810 [1852]
2. Height: 5'7½" [in 1831] 5'9" [in 1852]; "negro man of dark complexion with no visible mark or scar" [1831]; "man of black complexion" with "scar on outer corner of left eye" [1852]
3. Born free in Isle of Wight County [VA]
4. Isle of Wight County, April 14, 1831; Norfolk, April 2, 1833 and February 18, 1852
5. July 28, 1851 and July 31, 1858
6. "Zadock" Baker, age 40, appears in the City of Norfolk in the census of 1850 as a "mulatto" laborer, living alone. He could read and write.

BANKS, ELIZABETH
(Daughter of Benjamin and Nancy Banks)

1. Born circa 1799
2. Height: 5'4"; "Bright complexion, no scars or marks perceivable, full face"
3. Born free in Surry County "as appears by a former register obtained from John Faulcon, clerk"
4. Surry County, May 24, 1834
5. September 22, 1834

BANKS, JOHN
(Son of Elizabeth Banks)

1. Born circa 1816
2. Height: 5'8"; "Mulatto man" with "small scar behind right ear, also one on right arm, near elbow, full face, large nostrils"
3. Born free in Surry County, "as appears by a certificate from James Wilson"
4. Surry County, May 24, 1834
5. September 22, 1834

BANKS, MARY ANN

1. Born circa 1833
2. Height: 5'3" "Girl of mulatto complexion" with "scar on left side of chin"
3. Born free in Norfolk, proved by oath of John Palmer
4. Norfolk, March 11, 1850
5. July 26, 1858
6. Miss Banks for many years lived with her brother, Anthony Portlock and his family.
See Portlock, Anthony

BARBER, JAMES

1. Born circa 1807
2. Height: 5'7"; "Black man [with] scar on his under lip, occasioned by a cut, only one eye, being blind in the left eye, teeth sound, white, of square make."
3. "Emancipated by Courtney Brough [?] by will 12 May 1841, Elizabeth City County, recorded 27 November 1845."
4. Elizabeth City County, April 23, 1847
5. April 25, 1849

BARNES, MARTHA
"daughter of Lucinda Barnes"

1. Born circa 1824
2. Height: 5'1½"; "a free negro woman of black complexion; small black mole on right cheek."

3. Born free in Surry County, "having moved to this city to labor."
4. Norfolk City, April 25, 1848
5. July 30, 1853

BARRAUD, JOHN

1. Born circa 1828
2. Height: 5'1¼" [at 19]; "free boy of bright mulatto complexion" with "small mole near right corner of mouth and one on upper lip near right nostril" and "straight black hair"
3. Emancipated in Norfolk County by deed of C.W. Diggs
4. Norfolk, December 21, 1841 and April 14, 1847
5. July 27, 1858
6. "Child of JUSTINE BARRAUD, an emancipated slave"

BARRAUD, JOHNSON

1. Born circa 1834
2. _____
3. Born free
4. Norfolk County, June 20, 1836
5. 1842

BARRAUD, JUSTINE

1. Circa 1809
2. Height 5½, "A mulatto woman...with a scar on her right arm from a snag and a small scar between the forward and middle finger of her left hand"
3. "Emancipated by deed from C.W. Diggs, dated 20 September 1831 and recorded in the Court of Norfolk County"
4. Norfolk County, June 20, 1836
5. 1842
6. The Death Register for Norfolk, VA records the passing of "Justin Barrand" on January 18, 1871

BASS, ELIZA ANN

1. Born circa 1823
2. Height: 5'9½"; "Mulatto [with] small scar on left wrist, small scar on left arm a little above wrist, a scar on this wrist, a scar on the fore and two middle fingers of the left hand, just below the first knuckle joints."
3. Born free
4. Middlesex County, April 29, 1848
5. March 26, 1849

BATEMAN, SARAH ANN

1. Born circa 1824
2. Height: 5'3¾"; "a free girl, bright mulatto complexion"; "green eyes" and "no scar on head, face, or hands"
3. Born free in North Carolina, as proved by James Cherry
4. Norfolk, September 11, 1843
5. July, 1853

BELL, ANN

1. Circa 1822
2. Height: 5'4½"; "Woman of dark complexion [with] black mole and scar on left cheek, from a cut"
3. Born free
4. Norfolk County, March 15, 1847
5. February 25, 1850

BELL, BETHENIA

1. Circa 1818
2. Height 5'1". "Bright mulatto with small scar near left corner of left eye and scar on left wrist"
3. Not stated
4. Norfolk County, February 19, 1844
5. February 25, 1850

BELL, JAMES

1. Born circa 1828

2. Height 5'11"; "Man of dark complexion [with] no apparent marks or scars"
3. Not stated
4. Norfolk County, December 17, 1849
5. February 25, 1850

BELL, JAMES
(Son of Sally Bell)

1. Born circa 1841
2. Height: 5'4¾"; "Negro boy of black complexion" with "no apparent mark or scar on head, face, or hands"
3. Born free in Norfolk, proved by John Benjamin "of a female who was herself born free"
4. Norfolk, August 7, 1857
5. August 24, 1858

BELL, JENNY

1. Born circa 1796
2. Height 5'4¾, "A woman of light complexion...with no apparent marks or scars."
3. Born free in Norfolk County, "and has removed from the county of Norfolk to this borough [Norfolk] to labor herein"
4. Norfolk County, September 19, 1842; Norfolk, January 18, 1843
5. July 25, 1853

BELL, LEMUEL

1. Born circa 1797
2. Height: 5'8½"; "negro man of dark complexion" with "scar over left eye on the forehead"
3. Born free in Norfolk County
4. Norfolk County, October 17, 1836; Norfolk, May 31, 1837
5. May 27, 1837 and July 27, 1858
6. The U.S. Census of 1850 shows Lemuel Bell, age 74, "black", an "oysterman" living in Norfolk City with his Sarah, age 54, "black", and James 17, "black", and Martha, 14, "black".
Lemuel is the only member of the family group with an occupation listed. James and Martha could read and write, but Lemuel and

Sarah could not.

BELL, MARTHA
(Child of Sally Bell, "free mulatto woman")

1. Born circa 1837
2. Height: 5' [at 14]; "negro girl of black complexion" with "scar on left cheek"
3. Born free
4. Norfolk, July 28, 1851
5. July 26, 1858
6. Miss Bell, age 14, was enumerated in the U.S. Census of 1850 in Norfolk City with her parents, Lemuel, the oysterman, and Sarah, and her brother James, 17. They were all listed as "black."

BELL, SARAH

1. Born circa 1824 or 1826
2. Height: 5'5"; "Dark mulatto woman [with] scar on left side of face, near corner of mouth, from a burn [1847]; "negro woman of a dark mulatto complexion, scar on left side of face, near corner of mouth, from a burn" [1851]
3. Born free in Norfolk County, "removed therefrom to this city to labour therein"
4. Norfolk County, December 20, 1847; Norfolk, November 10, 1851
5. February 25, 1850 and July 28, 1858

BERRY, JAMES
(Son of Jane Berry)

1. Born circa 1832
2. Height: 4'3½" (he was 11); "free boy of bright mulatto complexion with blue eyes and a small scar on left cheek"
3. Born free in Norfolk, proved by James Hunter
4. Norfolk Borough, January 25, 1843
5. May 25, 1852

BERRY, JANE WILSON

1. Born circa 1811
2. Height: 5'; "Free woman of bright mulatto complexion" with "blue eyes" and "no apparent marks or scars"
3. Born free in Norfolk, proved by oath of William W. Sharp
4. Norfolk, July 13, 1852 Previous register "accidentally lost or destroyed"
5. January 28, 1861
6. On October 9, 1850, in the City of Norfolk, the U.S. Census found Jane Berry, 38, female, mulatto, living, doubtless as a servant, in the household of Edward P. Tabb, a 38 year old white merchant with real estate valued at $5200.

BERRY, MARTHA (alias Martha White) (see WHITE, MARTHA)

BERRY, SALLY (alias Sally Langley, Sally Wallace)

1. Born circa 1796
2. Height: 5'4" [in 1836]; 5'3 and one eighth [in 1851]; "free woman of yellow complexion with two small scars on back of left hand" [in 1845]; "free woman of color of yellow complexion with two small scars on the back of the left hand and a small mole on the right side of the nose" [1851]
3. Born free in Norfolk, proved by oath of Robert Langley
4. Norfolk, July 26, 1836 and June 4, 1851
5. May 26, 1851 and July 26, 1858

BINS, EDMUND

1. Born circa 1816
2. Height: 5'10': "Mulatto man, scar between left thumb and forefinger, scar on ring finger of right hand."
3. Born free in Goochland County.
4. Richmond, October 10, 1842
5. May 24, 1848

BLATT, PAULINE

1. Born circa 1832
2. Height: 4'10"; "mulatto girl" with "scar near the second joint of the thumb on the left hand, considerably freckled in the face"

3. Emancipated in Norfolk by deed of Nicholas Baueleur, June 24, 1846
4. Norfolk, October 26, 1849
5. June, 1855

BLIGH, ALICE

1. Born circa 1806
2. Height: 5'4¼"; "woman of mulatto complexion" with "scar on the nose, just below eyes" and missing "first joint of first finger of right hand"
3. Emancipated in Norfolk by will of Ann J. Woodson, December 23, 1806
4. Norfolk, March 12, 1850
5. July 26, 1858

BLIZZARD, IRENA

1. Born circa 1813
2. Height: 5'1¾"; "mulatto complexion" with "small scar on her neck, occasioned by a burn."
3. Born free in Surry County, "having removed therefrom to this city to labor therein."
4. Norfolk, March 27, 1847
5. July 28, 1853

BLUFORD, ELLENORA, see WALKER, ELLENORA

BLUFORD, WALTER, see WALKER, WALTER

BOBEE, ROSALIE

1. Born circa 1832
2. Height: 5'3¾"; "very bright mulatto complexion" and "no apparent marks or scars"
3. Born free in Norfolk, proven by oath of James Arbuthnot
4. Norfolk, October 7, 1847
5. September, 1858
6. "Rosalie is allowed to go at large till the next court, September 15, 1858, Wm W Lamb, Mayor"

Miss Bobee may have been living—as white—in Baltimore, in 1850. On July 10 of that year, in the 15th Ward of Baltimore, the census-taker enumerated the following family:

Joseph F. Bobee, 48, male, white, grocer, born Santo Domingo

Margaret Bobee, 35, female, white, born Virginia
Rosalie Bobee, age 19, female, white, born Virginia
John Bobee, age 15, male, white, born Santo Domingo
Joseph Bobee, age 9, male, white, born Maryland
William S. Bobee, age 5, male, white, born Maryland
Mary Bobee, age 2, female, white, born Maryland
Margaret Bobee, age 1, female, white, born Maryland
Ann Darragh, age 70, female, white, born Virginia, real estate valued at $3000

As of September, 1870, the mother had evidently died, but the father, Joseph, now 69, was still living in Baltimore, with sons James, 33, Joseph 28, and William 25, and daughters Margaret, 20, and Ellen 18. They were still listed as "white".

BONAR, JOSEPHINE
(Child of Cinderella Bonar)

1. Born circa 1836
2. Height not taken [She was 11 in 1847]; 5'1 and five eighths" [in 1853, at 17]; "Girl of bright mulatto complexion" with "mole on left cheek and one on chin" [1847]; "Free girl of bright mulatto complexion, mole on left cheek and one on chin and freckles on the face" [1853]
3. Born free in Norfolk, by oath of Elizabeth Cullumbrass (?)
4. Norfolk, December 24, 1847 and August 11, 1853
5. July 26, 1853 and December 3, 1859

BONAR, ROBERT
(Child of Cinderella Bonar)

1. Born February, 1847
2. Height not taken; "mulatto complexion"
3. Born free in Norfolk, by oath of Elizabeth Cullumbrass (?)
4. Norfolk, December 24, 1847
5. July 26, 1853

BOROUGH, MARY

1. Born circa 1820
2. Height 5'4¾, "Negro woman of black complexion...no scar"
3. Born free in Southampton County
4. Southampton County, May 15, 1841
5. January 2, 1847

BORUM, DAVID

1. Born circa 1810
2. Height: 5'8"; "Free man of bright mulatto complexion" with "small scar between eyes"
3. Born free in Norfolk, proved by oath of Louisa Short
4. Norfolk, April 26, 1837 and October 10, 1853
5. February 1, 1861
6. David Borum, "black", age 69 and his wife, Ellen, "mulatto", age 55, appear in the census on 29 National Street in Norfolk on June 14, 1880. Borum was working as a laborer.

BOUSH, CHARLES

1. Born circa 1789
2. Height: 5'6¼"; "Negro man with a scar on the upper part of his forehead"
3. Emancipated by will of William Boush, deceased, recorded in Princess Anne County, February 3, 1834
4. Princess Anne County, June 5, 1837
5. February 25, 1850

BOUSH, DANIEL
(Son of Sally Boush)

1. Born circa 1834
2. Height: 5'1¼" [at 16]; "Mulatto boy" with "mark or scar on chin, scar over left eye, and small one on middle finger of left hand"
3. Born free in Norfolk, proven by oath of David M. Walke
4. Norfolk, February 25, 1850
5. July 23, 1855

6. The U.S. Census of 1850 shows that Daniel Boush was part of a large family living in Norfolk City in August:

Sarah [i.e. Sally] Boush, 42, female, black   Value of real estate: $750

Daniel Boush, 16, male, black, Labourer
Thomas Boush, 12, male, black
Mary S. Boush, 11, female, black
John Boush, 8, male, black
Martha F. Boush, 4, female, black
Wm. Henry Boush, 1, male black
Nancy Boush, 30, female, black
Mary L. Boush, 12, female, black
Cornelius Boush, 2, male, black
Margaret Boush, 6 months, female, black

Nancy could neither read nor write.

BOUSH, GEORGE

1. Born circa 1810
2. Height: 5'3½"; "Dark complected negro with a scar on right leg and another on left leg."
3. Emancipated by will of William Boush, deceased, recorded in Princess Anne County, February 3, 1834
4. Princess Anne County, June 5, 1837
5. February 25, 1850

BOUSH, JACK
(Son of Lettuce [sic] Boush)

1. Born circa 1835
2. Height: 4'8½" [he was 15]; "Negro boy of black complexion" with "deep scar on the left jaw and the forefinger and middle finger of his right hand cut off"
3. Born free in Norfolk, proved by oath of David M. Walke
4. Norfolk, February 25, 1850
5. July 26, 1858

BOUSH, JASPER

1. Born circa 1815

2. Height: 5'9" "in shoes"; "Light complected negro without any apparent mark or scar, except very much marked with the smallpox in the face."
3. Emancipated by the will of William Boush, deceased, Princess Anne County.
4. Princess Anne County, December 7, 1846
5. September 25, 1848

BOUSH, JOHN, see BOUSH, DANIEL and BOUSH, SALLY

BOUSH, LAVINIA
(Daughter of Sally Boush, alias Whitfield)

1. Born circa 1825
2. Height: 5'; "free girl of light black complexion" with "small scar on forehead and one on right arm near elbow"
3. Emancipated by Robert B. Stark, by deed, February 7, 1838
4. Norfolk, January 24, 1843
5. July 26, 1856
6. Lavinia Boush had a son, Edward Boush, "a mulatto child one year old, born free in Norfolk [circa 1842].

BOUSH, LETTICE

1. Circa 1813
2. Height 5', "A dark complected negro woman, without any apparent mark or scar" [1834]: "Free negro woman of black complexion" with "small scar on upper lip, near right corner of mouth"
3. "Emancipated by the will of William Boush, deceased, Court of Princess Anne, recorded the 3rd day of February, 1834."
4. Princess Anne County, May 5, 1834; Norfolk, March 9, 1844
5. August 22, 1842 and July 26, 1858
6. "Lettuce" Boush appears in the U.S. Census of 1850. She is described as 40 years old and "black", with no occupation listed. With her are children Phillis, 22; Susan, 19; Philip 18, and Jack, 16. Mary, age 24, is living next door. She also appears in the census of 1860, taken in the city of Norfolk on July 31st of that year. Her age is given as 48, her color as black. No occupation is given for her, but her son Philip, 24, black, is a "drayman" and her daughter Susan, age

20, black, is a "laundress." Living with them also was Abram Boush, a ten year old black male, who must have been born after the 1850 census.

BOUSH, MARTHA FRANCES, see BOUSH, DANIEL and BOUSH, SALLY

BOUSH, MARY

1. Born circa 1821
2. Height not given in 1834; 5'3½ [1850]; "Dark complected negro girl [with] a scar on her forehead and one on her left hand near wrist [1834]: "negro woman of black complexion" with "scar on her forehead and one on her left hand, near the wrist" [1850]
3. Emancipated by the will of William Boush, Princess Anne County, February 3, 1834
4. Princess Anne County, May 5, 1834; Norfolk, March 4, 1850, "having removed from said county to this city to labour therein"
5. February 15, 1850 and July 26, 1858

BOUSH, MARY LOUISA
(Granddaughter of Sally Boush, alias Whitfield)

1. Born circa 1838
2. Height not taken [when she was seven] 5'1½" [at 16]; "free negro girl of black complexion" with "no apparent mark or scar on face, head, or hands"
3. Emancipated in Norfolk Borough by Robert B. Stark, by deed, February 27, 1838
4. Norfolk, February 20, 1843 and April 10, 1854
5. March 29, 1854 and January 3, 1861
6. See the entry for Daniel Boush.

BOUSH, MARY SUSAN

1. Born circa 1840
2. Height: 4'7" [she was 10]; 5'3¾ [at 15]; "mulatto girl" with "mole on right side of her neck, just above collar bone" [1850]; "Free girl of mulatto complexion" with "mole on right side of neck and scar on left arm below elbow, occasioned by a burn"

3. Born free in Norfolk, proved by oath of David M. Walke
4. Norfolk, February 25, 1850 and November 5, 1855
5. July 23, 1855 and October 23, 1860
6. See Boush, Daniel

[BOUSH], NANCY[2]

1. Circa 1818
2. Height: 5'¼; "Black woman without any mark or scar"
3. Emancipated by the will of William Boush, Princess Anne County.
4. Princess Anne County, May 4, 1840
5. February 25, 1850
6. She appears in the 1850 census in the household of 42 year old Sarah Boush (perhaps a sister).
Nancy was perhaps a younger sister of Sarah.

BOUSH, PHILIP

1. Circa 1832
2. Height 2'5"[in 1834]; 5'3" [at 18 in 1850], "A dark complected negro boy...without any apparent mark or scar" [1834]; "Negro boy

---

[2] Registrants are occasionally listed only by their given names (or nicknames). In this case "Nancy", liberated by one William Boush, can be located in the 1850 census alone, with other members of the family, as a daughter of Sarah ("Sally") Bush.

of black complexion" with "no apparent mark or scar"

3. Emancipated by the will of William Boush, Princess Anne County, February 3, 1834 [1834]; "Born free in Norfolk, proved by David M. Walke" [1850]
4. Princess Anne County, May 5, 1834; Norfolk, March 4, 1850
5. August 22, 1842 and July 26, 1858
6. See Boush, Lettice

BOUSH, PHILLIS

1. Circa 1827
2. Height 3'10" [at seven in 1834]; 5'2" [at 21 in 1848 and 23 in 1850]; "A dark complected negro girl, lame in the left hip" [1834]; "Black woman, lame in left hip, occasioned by disease, no apparent mark or scar" [1848];"Negro woman of black complexion, lame in left hip" with "no apparent marks or scars" [1850]
3. Emancipated by the will of William Boush, deceased, Princess Anne County, February 3, 1834
4. Princess Anne County, May 5, 1834 and December 4, 1848; Norfolk, March 4, 1850
5. August 22, 1842, December 5, 1848 and July 26, 1858
6. See Boush, Lettice

BOUSH, SALLY (SARAH)

1. Circa 1801-1802
2. Height: 5'3¼" [1837 and 1850]; 5'3 and one eighth" [1855]; "Negro woman of light black complexion" with "scar on left thumb" [1837 and 1850]; "Free negro woman of light black complexion" with "scar on left thumb near first joint"
3. Emancipated in Princess Anne County [VA] by will of William Boush, deceased, recorded in Princess Anne County, February 3, 1834, "removed therefrom to this city to labour therein"
4. Princess Anne County, June 5, 1837; Norfolk, March 4, 1850 and November 5, 1855
5. February 25, 1850, July 23, 1855, and October 23, 1860
6. She was registered along with the following children:

John, age 8 (born circa 1842), "boy of black complexion with a small scar near corner of left eye"

Martha Frances, age 5 (born circa 1845), "girl of light black complexion with "no apparent mark or scar"

William Henry, age 2 (born circa 1848), "boy of light black complexion" with no apparent mark or scar"

See Boush, Daniel and Whitfield, Lavinia

BOUSH, SUSAN
("Daughter of Lettuce [sic] Boush")

1. Circa 1830
2. Height 3' [in 1834, age 4]; 4'10¾" [in 1850, age 20]; "A dark complected negro girl, without any apparent mark or scar" [1834]; "Negro girl of black complexion" with "scar near left corner of mouth" [1850]
3. Emancipated by will of William Boush, deceased, Princess Anne County, February 3, 1834 [1834]; "Born free in Norfolk County, by oath of David M. Walke" [1850]
4. Princess Anne County, May 5, 1834; Norfolk, March 4,1850
5. August 22, 1842 and July 28, 1858

BOUSH, TONEY

1. Circa 1828
2. Height: 5'7"; "Mulatto man with a mole on right hand."
3. Emancipated by will of William Boush, deceased, Princess Anne County.
4. Princess Anne County, June 4, 1849
5. February 25, 1850

BOUSH, WILLIAM HENRY, see BOUSH, DANIEL and BOUSH, SALLY

BOWDOIN, NANCY, see HUNTER, MARY ANN

BOWMAN, DAVID

1. Born circa 1810
2. Height: 5'8½"; "Free man of colour of mulatto complexion" with "scar on back of left hand and mole on nose between his eyes"
3. Born free in Norfolk, on oath of Louisa Shittle
4. Norfolk, April 26, 1837
5. July 26, 1853

BOWYER, ELIZA

1. Born circa 1820
2. Height: 4'9"; "Negro woman of dark complexion with no apparent mark or scar on head, face, or hands"
3. Born free in Isle of Wight County [VA], "removed from said county to this city to labor therein"
4. Norfolk, April 25, 1848
5. July 30, 1853

BOWZER, GEORGE (of)[3]

1. Circa 1807
2. Height 5'8½", "Yellow man [with] no apparent mark or scar" [1831]. Upon second registration [1842] "he now has a very small scar at the left corner of the left eye."
3. Born free
4. Nansemond County, July 11, 1842; Norfolk, July 1, 1845
5. September 22, 1851
6. "Thomas Bowser, late of Nansemond County, was well known to me as an honest and well-behaved man of color. He is the father of the bearer George Bowser, who I have reason also to believe is a man of honesty and respectability." (Richard H. Baker, June 23d, '45)"

BOYD, ANN

---

[3]

The Clerk of Nansemond County had the habit of attaching the suffix "of" to the surname of his registrants

(Daughter of Nancy Boyd)

1. Born circa 1815-1816
2. Height: 5'2½" [in 1846], 5'2 and five eighths [1853]; "Free negro woman of black complexion" with "small scar on upper lip, near left corner of the mouth, a small one near right corner of right eye, and one on back of left wrist"
3. Born free in Norfolk
4. Norfolk, December 1, 1846 and November 2, 1853
5. July 26, 1853 and January 28, 1861
6. "She is the descendant of a female Negro born free before the first day of May, 1806" (Clerk, 1853)
   "Required to apply to next court for renewal, January 18, 1861, Wm. W. Lamb, Mayor"

BOYD, MARIA
(Daughter of Nancy Boyd)

1. Born circa 1812
2. Height: 5'¾"; "Free negro woman of black complexion" with "scar on the right side of nose, three scars in left arm, near wrist, and three scars on right arm between wrist and elbow"
3. Born free in Norfolk
4. Norfolk, February 23, 1850
5. July 26, 1858

BOYD, NANCY

1. Born circa 1789
2. Height: 4'10¾"; "Free negro woman of black complexion" with "scar on right cheek and one near the end of the ring finger of right hand, which has stiffened the last joint of that finger."
3. Born free in Norfolk
4. Norfolk August 3, 1835 and December 1, 1846
5. July 26, 1853

BOYD, SYLVIA
(Daughter of Nancy Boyd)

1. Born circa 1810
2. Height: 5'¼"; "Free Negro woman of black complexion" with "small scar on the underlip, near right center of mouth, one on forehead, just at edge of hair, and near left temple."
3. Born free in Norfolk City
4. Norfolk, August 31, 1832
5. July 26, 1853

BRANCH, JESSE

1. Born circa 1820
2. Height 5'8", "Negro man of light complexion, small scar on nose, directly between eyes"
3. "Free parentage"
4. Isle of Wight County, January 4, 1841
5. April 28, 1843

BRANCH, SALLY

1. Born circa 1811
2.. Height: 5'3"; "negro woman of dark complexion with small scar on the right wrist, near the hand"
3. Born of free parents in Isle of Wight County, VA
4. Isle of Wight County, January 4, 1832; Norfolk Borough, September 4, 1834

BRISTER [No surname], see Rudd, Brister

BROADWATER, JAMES

1. Born circa 1817
2. Height: 5'6¾"; "Nearly black, with a scar on left wrist, occasioned by cuts."
3. Born free
4. Middlesex County, August 10, 1848
5. March 26, 1849

BROWN, BETSEY

1. Born circa 1805
2. Height: 5'2"; "Negro woman of light complexion, small scar on right eyebrow, black mole on left side of nose"
3. Emancipated in the City of Norfolk by Jonas Brown, by deed dated November 24, 1845
4. Norfolk City, December 2, 1845
5. August 30, 1851

BROWN, DIANA
(Daughter of Sally Pollard)

1. Born circa 1829
2. Height: 4'10½"; "Woman of mulatto complexion, scar on thumb of left hand"
3. Born free in Norfolk, prove by oath of William W. Sharp
4. Norfolk, April 3, 1850
5. March 24, 1858

BROWN, JAMES

1. Born circa 1800
2. Height: 5'2¾" [1840], 5'2¼ [1851]; "Man of dark complexion" with "no apparent mark or scar" [1840]; "Negro man of black complexion" with "small scar near left eyebrow" [1851]
3. Emancipated by John W. Murdaugh, esq., January 1, 1836
4. Norfolk, March 5, 1840 and September 4, 1851
5. March 18, 1840 and January 28, 1861

BROWN, JONAS

1. Born circa 1800
2. Height: 5'2¾"; "A free negro man of dark complexion, having a small scar near the left eyebrow"
3. Emancipated by John Wellington, Esquire, of Norfolk County by deed, bearing date of January 1, 1836
4. Norfolk, May 28, 1840
5. August 30, 1851
6. The U.S. Census of 1850 shows Jonas Brown, age 49, "black", working as a laborer in the City of Norfolk. He was living with Elizabeth Brown, age 44, "black", evidently his wife, and Joseph

Byrd, age 13, "black." None of the three could read or write.

BROWN, ROSANNA BRYAN

1. Born circa 1809
2. Height: 5'2"[in 1839]; 5'1½" [in 1853]: "Negro woman of black complexion with mark on right cheekbone, occasioned by a sting of a bee, scar on second finger of left hand"
3. Emancipated January 15, 1839, by deed from Eugene N. Bobee
4. Norfolk, December 4, 1839 and August 8, 1853
5. 1853 and July 26, 1858

BUCK, LOUISA

1. Born circa 1803
2. Height: 5'8¼"; "Negro woman of black complexion, with no marks or scars on her head, face, or hands"
3. Born free in Southampton County [VA]
4. Norfolk Borough, August 29, 1835
5. November 24, 1851
6. Louisa Bucks was enumerated in the Census of 1850 in Norfolk City. Her age was given as "35"—12 years younger than the age given in her freedom papers. She was living with 28 year old Richard Ricks. No occupation is given for either. Both were described as "black" and illiterate.
See: Burrows, Dick

BULL, LYDIA

1. Born circa 1785
2. Height 5'2½", "A woman of black complexion...with a small scar near the left wrist, the left thumb defective"
3. Emancipated by the will of Franklin Bull of the Parish of St. George in the County of Accomack, July 11, 1809
4. Accomack County, July 27, 1841
5. August 22, 1842
6. Lydia Bull, according to the U.S. Census of 1850, age 65, black, illiterate, was living alone in "Norfolk City."

BURROWS, DICK (ALIAS RICKS)

1. Born circa 1821
2. Height: 5'1¾" [at 23]; "negro man of dark complexion" with "fingers of right hand deformed and compacted, said to be occasioned by burn"
3. Born free in Southampton County [VA]
4. Southampton County, January 8, 1844
5. August 3, 1858
6. Richard Ricks was enumerated in Norfolk in the 1850 census. He was described as 28 years old and black and living with Louisa Buck, who was 35 and black. No occupation was listed for either. Neither could read or write.

BURROWS, EMMA JANE
(Daughter of Ann Boyd)

1. Born circa 1832
2. Height: 4'11" ; "Negro girl of light mulatto complexion" with "scar in middle of forehead, small scar on back of hand"
3. Born free in Norfolk
4. Norfolk, June 7, 1853
5. July 26, 1858
6. "I am unable to state whether or not she is a descendant of a female slave emancipated since first day of May 1806" (Clerk)
    See: Boyd, Ann and Boyd, Nancy

BURT, MARY ANTOINETTE

1. Born circa 1817
2. Height: 5'1½"[at 17]; "Bright mulatto girl" with "mole on chin and red hair"
3. Born free in Norfolk
4. Norfolk, October 1, 1826 and August 8, 1835
5. July 26, 1858
BYRD, ALEXANDER
(Child of Maria Byrd)

1. Born 1833
2. Height: 4'7¾" [he was 12]; "Negro boy, light black complexion, with a scar in the right eyebrow."

3. Emancipated by last will and testament of Horatio Moore, deceased, in County of Prince George [VA], proved by oath of Horatio Moore

4. Norfolk, August 23, 1842; November 12, 1845

5. September 25, 1851

See Byrd, Maria

BYRD, JOSEPH
(Child of Maria Byrd)

1. Born 1836

2. Height: 4½" [he was 10]; "Negro boy of light black complexion" with "a black mole on the right temple and a small scar near the outer corner of the left eye."

3. Born free in Prince George County [VA], proved by oath of Horatio Moore

4. Norfolk, August 23, 1842; November 12, 1845

5. September 25, 1851

6. The U.S. Census of 1850 shows a 13 year old Joseph Byrd, "black", living in Norfolk City with Jonas and Elizabeth Brown.

See Byrd, Maria

BYRD, MARIA

1. Circa 1812

2. Height: 5'3" [in 1836]; 5'2¾"[in 1842], "Of bright complexion"... "has a scar on the left hand and another on the left arm"

3. Emancipated by the will of Horatio Moore of City Point, Prince George County, January 12, 1836

4. Prince George County, 1836; Norfolk, August 23, 1842

5. September 25, 1851

6. "Ages of my children:

      Emily Morris was born at City Point, February 10, 1830

      Elexander [sic] Bird [sic] was born at City Point, March 31, 1833

      Joseph Bird was born at City Point, February 23, 1836

CALLIS, ELLEN
(Daughter of Mary Ann Callis)

1. Born circa 1837
2. Height: 4'8" [she was 13]; "black complexion" with "scar on forehead and scar on left shoulder"
3. Born free in Norfolk, proved by oath of Mary J. Hughes
4. Norfolk, February 21, 1850
5. July 26, 1858
6. "Allowed to apply to next Court, Wm. W. Lamb, Mayor, July 26, 1858"
Her name was Ellenora, and she appeared with her mother and five siblings in the U.S. Census of Norfolk in 1850.

CALLIS, JANE
(Daughter of Mary Ann Callis)

1. Born circa 1833
2. Height: 5'½"; "Free negro girl of light black complexion" with "scar over the left eye, near brow"
3. Born free in Norfolk, proven by oath of Mary J. Hughes
4. Norfolk, July 23, 1838 and February 21, 1850
5. July 26, 1858

CALLIS, MARY ANN

1. Born circa 1808
2. Height: 5'3½"; "Negro woman of light black complexion" with "scar on the wrist of right arm and another scar on same arm above elbow and several small scars about the forehead and face"
3. Emancipated in Mathews County [VA] by last will and testament of Joh Callis, deceased"; "removed therefrom to this city to labour therein"
4. Norfolk, February 21, 1850
5. July 28, 1858
6. Mary Ann Callis appears in the U.S. Census of 1850 in Norfolk City, along with her six children: Jane, 13; Ellenora, 12; John H. 9; Georgiana, 8; Lucy Ann, 5; and William, 3. No occupation is given for Mrs. Callis. She and all her children are described as "black."

CALLIS, SARAH ELIZABETH

1. Born circa 1822

1. Born circa 1828
2. Height: 5'3 and seventh eights"; "Negro boy of very light complexion, near white, with straight hair and grey or blue eyes" and "no apparent marks or scars"
3. Born free in Norfolk, proved by oath of William Holmes
4. Norfolk, June 6, 1850
5. May 26, 1858
6. John Carter, male, mulatto, single, age 52, was enumerated in the U.S. Census in the City of Norfolk on June 3, 1880. He was a servant of Bailey Adams and was working as a wheelwright.

On the 8th of June, 1900, the census takers found him, at the age of 72, in the Norfolk City Almshouse in Kempsville, in Princess Anne County. His month of birth is given as June, 1828.

CARTER, WILLIAM

1. Born circa 1827
2. Height 5'8" "in shoes", "Mulatto [with] scar on the right arm, occasioned by a burn, no other marks or scars perceivable"
3. Born of free parents
4. Williamsburg, December 31, 1846
5. February 22, 1847

_____, CATHARINE
("Daughter of Esther")

1. Born circa 1816
2. Height 5'½"; "Free woman of bright complexion" with "scar in right eyebrow"
3. Born free in Norfolk
4. Norfolk, February 21, 1850
5. July 26, 1858
6. "Allowed to go at large until next Court, Wm W Lamb, Mayor, July 21, 1858"

_____, CELIA [Surname not given]

1. Born circa 1811

2. Height: 5'4 and one eighths; "Negro woman of black complexion" with "scar under the right eye"
3. Born free in the City of Williamsburg
4. Norfolk, February 20, 1850
5. July 26, 1858
6. "Allowed to go at large until next Court, Wm. W. Lamb, Mayor, July 21, 1858"

CHALK, MILLY (of)

1. Born October 10, 1807
2. Height 5'2"; "Woman of brown complexion [with] no apparent mark or scar"
3. Born free
4. Nansemond County, October 12, 1835, renewed August 9, 1847
5. February 26, 1850

CHAPMAN, SARAH ANN COSSA

1. Born circa 1822
2. Height: 5'4½" ; "Negro woman of brown complexion" with "small scar on thumb of right hand"
3. Born free in Norfolk
4. Norfolk, April 2, 1850
5. July 27, 1858
6. Mrs. Chapman had two daughters:
   Olivia Frances Chapman
   Born circa 1844
   "Child of brown complexion"
   Born free in Norfolk

   Laura Virginia Chapman
   Born circa 1847
   "Child of brown complexion" with "mole on left corner of upper lip"
   Born free in Norfolk

CHAPPELL, HENRY

1. Born circa 1817

2. Height: 5'2"; "Yellow complexion, no scar"
3. Born free in Southampton County
4. Southampton County, May 15, 1843
5. January 28, 1850

CHAPPELL, SIMON

1. Born circa 1823
2. Height 5'3¾"; "Black man [with] scar on nose and left forefinger"
3. Born free in Southampton County
4. Southampton County, April 14, 1849
5. February 25, 1850

CHAULK, CLARISSA

1. Born circa 1814
2. Height: 5'1"; "Woman of brown complexion, no apparent mark or scar."
3. Born free in Nansemond County, "removed from said county to this city to labor therein"
4. Nansemond County, registry renewed February 14, 1848; Norfolk, February 19, 1850
5. July 23, 1849 and July 26, 1858

CHURCHWARD, MARY

1. Born circa 1827
2. Height: 5'2"; "Mulatto [with] small scar near center of forehead and small scars on the left cheek, from cuts, a scar on back of right hand from a burn, small scar near first join of forefinger of left hand, from cut."
3. Born free
4. Norfolk County, October 15, 1849
5. October 26, 1849

CLAYTON, MOSES

1. ____
2. ____
3. ____

4.____
5. February 10, 1842

"State of Maryland
City of Baltimore, to wit
on the tenth day of February one thousand eight
hundred forty two before the Subscriber a Justice of the peace of the
State of Maryland in and for the City aforesaid personally appeared
Moses Clayton (Col'd) and made oath on the Holy Evangely [sic] of
Almighty God, that on the 5th day of September 1841 he lost in the
City of Washing [sic] near the Capitol, by the foot path of the canal
and near the Glass house a large Brown leather Pocket Book,
containing the following articles, namely, Moses Clayton's free
papers and those of his ordination as minister of the Gospel, and
others relative to the incorporation of the church of which he is
Pastor in the city of Baltimore, also three dollars one which was a
Rail Road note, also his Wife's free papers Having thereon the
Names of her two daughters, Margaret Ann, and Rosanna, which
papers and property is yet undiscovered and not obtained by this
deponent, or any other person to his knowledge and belief,
subscribed and sworn to before me, James Blair J[ustice of the]
Peace
Moses Clayton

State of Maryland City of Baltimore to Wit on the tenth day
of February 1842 before the Subscriber a Justice of the peace in and
for the City aforesaid personally appealed Eneas M. Saul, Merchant
of this City, and made oath on the Holy Evangely of Almighty God
that he has known Moses Clayton who has testified to the above
deposition, for the last 5 years and believing the facts he there
disposeth are true, this deponent further states that for integrity of
purpose, and Moral Honesty, he has always found Clayton above
suspicion.
Sworn and subscribed before James Blair J. Peace
Eneas M. Saul

State of Maryland
City of Baltimore to wit
I hereby certify that I have personal knowledge of Eneas M.
Saul, Merchant of this City who had signed and sworn to the within
deposition, and who is entitled to full faith and credit,

James Blair
Justice of Peace

State of Maryland
Baltimore County
  I hereby certify that James Blair Gentleman before whom the aforegoing affadavits were made who has thereto signed his name was at the time of so doing a Justice of the Peace of the State of Maryland and for the City of Baltimore duly commissioned and sworn In testimony whereof therefore I here taketh my hand and affix the seal of Baltimore County Court this 10th day of February 1842

Th R Kell, Clk

According to the U.S. Census of 1850, Moses Clayton was living as a free man in Baltimore. He is described as 50 years old, black, and a carpenter, with personal property valued at $1000. His wife, Susan, was 40 years old, and living in the household were the daughters Margaret, 20, and Rosanna, 17, as well as two other children, Bethanna, 10, and Isaac 4. In the Census of 1860, Clayton's age is given as 72 (with a birthdate around 1788), and his wife Susan is 55. Clayton is described as a Baptist minister with personal property valued at $600. His daughters, Margaret Mann and Susan Green are now married, and there is a one month old grandson, Moses Green.

CLEGG, WILLIAM HENRY

1. Born circa 1814
2. Height: 5'4¼"; "free man of mulatto complexion" with "scar on the throat"
3. Born free in Northampton County
4. Norfolk, July 9, 1847
5. July 26, 1858

_____CLEMENTINE
(see Lumlet, Clementine)

COCKE, CATY TYNES

1. Born circa 1787
2. Height: 5'4½"; "Mulatto woman"
3. Emancipated by last will and testament of Timothy Tynes of Isle of Wight County
4. Isle of Wight County, December 4, 1837
5. November 28, 1838

COLEMAN, TOM

1. Born circa 1800
2. Height: 5'4½; "Negro man of black complexion" with "small mark or scar on end of each of his little fingers"
3. "Emancipated in City of Norfolk by deed of Harriet H. Sanders, executrix of William Davis, deceased"
4. Norfolk, March 31, 1849
5. July 27, 1858

COLLINS, JIM

1. Circa 1822
2. Height: 5'2¼"; "Light black, no visible scars"
3. Born free in Accomack County
4. Accomack County, January 29, 1844
5. February 26, 1850

COLLINS, LOVEY

1. Born August 11, 1826
2. Height: 5'7 and 6/10ths"; "Chestnut color, scar from burn under right eye, small scar on left cheek, scar on inside of right wrist, black mole on upper part of left breast, prominent forehead, very likely."
3. Born free in Northampton County
4. Northampton County, May 14, 1850
5. May 30, 1850

COOK, ELIZABETH

1. Born circa 1822

2. Height: 4'9" [in 1835, at 13]; 5'2" [in 1838]; "Light complexion" with "scar on her right jaw" [1835]; "Negro girl of light complexion with a scar under her right jaw" [1838]
3. Born free in Norfolk County, "having removed from the said county to this borough to labor."
4. Norfolk County, September 21, 1835; Norfolk Borough, April 23, 1838
5. April 23, 1838 and July 25, 1853
See Cook, Polly (evidently her sister) and Willoughby, Nancy Cook (evidently her mother)

COOK, GEORGE

1. Born circa 1826
2. Height: 5'6½"; "Negro man of light black complexion" with "scar on the breast, near the neck"
3. Born free in Elizabeth City County [VA]
4. Norfolk, March 24, 1849
5. March 29, 1854
6. The U.S. Census of 1850 shows a George Cook, age 24, male, "black", living in Norfolk City on August 5. Living with him were 20 year old Georgianna Cook, and eight month old Hiram Cook, both "black," evidently his wife and son. George was a barber. He could not read or write, but Georgianna could.

COOK, POLLY

1. Born circa 1818
2. Height: 5'3" [1835], 5'2" [1853]; "Mulatto" with "scar on her neck from a burn" [1835]; "scar on her neck under the right jaw" [1853]
3. Born free in Norfolk County "having removed from the said county to this Borough to labour."
4. Norfolk County, September 21, 1835; Norfolk Borough, April 23, 1838
5. April 23, 1838 and July 25, 1853
6. Polly Cook, "black," age 38, appears in the U.S. Census of 1850 as the head of a household that included Caroline Gilmore, age 60, Thomas Whiting, 16, Sarah Jasper, 16, John Williams, 33, William Williams, 9, David Williams, 5, and Moses Williams, 2.

See Willoughby, Nancy Cook, who may have been her mother

COOKE, CHARLES
(Son of Betty Cooke, alias Betty Temers)

1. Born circa 1817
2. Height: 5'10¼"; "Mulatto man" with "scar on his forehead"
3. Born free in Norfolk
4. March 9, 1842
5. July, 1853

COOPER, CALEB

1. Born circa 1820
2. Height: 5'4½"; "Man of light complexion [with] no apparent marks or scars" [1842]; "Free man of bright mulatto complexion" with "scar on the ball of right thumb, occasioned by a rising"
3. Born free in Norfolk County "as appears from certificate of his registry granted by Clerk of Court of said County" [1849]
4. Norfolk County, May 16, 1842; Norfolk, August 27, 1849
5. August 28, 1848 and August 25, 1856

COOPER, MARY

1. Born circa 1824
2. Height 5'4¾", "A free woman of dark mulatto complexion" with a "scar on the second joint of the little finger of the right hand, a scar on the last joint of the forefinger of the left hand, and a mole on right cheek."
3. Born free in Norfolk County
4. Norfolk County, April 20, 1846; Norfolk, May 5, 1846
5. April 29, 1846 and July 25, 1853

COOPER, NANCY

1. Born circa 1795
2. Height: 4'11½"; "Negro woman of black complexion" with "no

apparent marks or scars"
3. Emancipated in Norfolk by will of Ann Camp, August 28, 1848
4. Norfolk, April 2, 1850
5. July 26, 1858
6. Nancy Cooper, female, mulatto, 53, was enumerated in the U.S. Census of 1850 in Norfolk City. She was living alone, but in the previous household lived Hannah Cornick, who was probably her mother, and Elizabeth Ruffin and Mary Cornick, who were probably her nieces.

COOPER, WILLIAM
(Register is badly deteriorated and in many places illegible)

2. Height: 5'6½"; "Free man of black complexion"
4. Norfolk, [   ]1853
5. July 26, 1858

COPELAND, CAROLINE (of)

1. Born circa 1814
2. Height 5'4", "A woman of brown complexion [with] no apparent mark or scar"
3. Free born
4. Nansemond County, September 27, 1836
5. February 22, 1847
6. The U.S. Census of 1850 shows Caroline Copeland, "female, black", as a member of the household of Joseph Bailey, a baker. According to the census, she was 29, indicating a birthdate closer to 1821 than 1814.

COPELAND, MARY FRANCES
("Child of Caroline Copeland, free woman of color")

1. Born circa 1839
2. Height: 4'8¾" [at 11]; "Negro girl of black complexion" with "small scar on the left side of her forehead and another small scar on the outer corner of her left eye"
3. Born free in Norfolk, proved by oath of Seana W. Thrift
4. Norfolk, June 12, 1850
5. June 28, 1860

COPELAND, VIRGINIA CAROLINA
("Child of Caroline Copeland, free woman of color")

1. Born circa 1841
2. Height 4'3 and seven eighths" [she was 9]; "Negro girl of light black complexion" with "scar on right arm, near shoulder"
3. Born free in Norfolk
4. Norfolk, June 12, 1850
5. July 26, 1858

COPELAND, WILLIAM HENRY (of)

1. Born circa 1825
2. Height: 5'3"; "Brown man [with] scar under each eye, one on palm of left hand and several on backs of both hands"
3. Born free
4. Richmond, October 21, 1846
5. February 27, 1850

CORNICK, JAMES

1. Born circa 1815
2. Height: 5'8"; "Man of dark complexion [with] no apparent mark on head or hands"
3. Born free
4. Norfolk Borough, October 7, 1836
5. August 28, 1849

CORNICK, MARY

1. Born circa 1818
2. Height: 4'10¼'; "negro woman of bright mulatto complexion" with "small scar in right arm above wrist"
3. Emancipated by will of Ann Camp, August 28, 1848
4. Norfolk, April 2, 1850
5. July 26, 1858
6. Mary Cornick, according to the U.S. Census of 1850, was living in the household of Elizabeth Ruffin, a former slave of Ann Camp, who had been emancipated at the same time. Living with them was

Thomas is also described as "idiotic."

CUFFEE, NANCY ANN

1. Born circa 1838
2. Height: 5'5½"; "Light complected negro woman" with "large burn or scar on the right arm"
3. Born free in Princess Anne County
4. Norfolk, October 5, 1857
5. December 28, 1850

DAVIS, MARTHA ANN (of)[4] (and Alfred, her child)

1. Born circa 1825
2. Height 4'11"... "A black woman...[with] several scars on right hand and one over right eye."
3. Emancipated by the last will of Robert Cox, deceased
4. Nansemond County, August 10, 1846
5. December 30, 1846

DAVIS, MARY ELIZA

1. Born May, 1841
2. Height: 4'11" [at 12]; "Girl of light complexion" with "no apparent mark or scar"
3. Born free in Norfolk
4. Norfolk, August 9, 1853
5. May 3, 1860
6. "I am unable to ascertain whether or not she is the descendant of a

---

[4] Joseph Prentis, County Clerk of Nansemond County, often prefixed the last names of his registrants with "of", as if to indicate the family by which they were originally owned, but Martha Davis' former master was a Cox.

female negro emancipated since first day of May 1806"

DAVIS, SUSAN

1. Born circa 1819
2. Height: 5'¾"; "Bright mulatto girl, stout made, thick bushy hair, round face, no visible scars on face or hands" [1839]; "bright mulatto" with "no apparent marks or scars on face, head, or hands" [1849]
3. Born free in Mathews County [VA]
4. Mathews County, September 9, 1839; Norfolk, October 30, 1849
5. October 22, 1849 and October 23, 1854
6. "Daughter of Nancy Davis, a white woman of the county."

DAWLEY, BETSEY

1. Born circa 1815-1816
2. Height: 5'; "Dark complected negro with bushy hair and a small scar on the back of the right wrist" [1837]; "Negro woman of black complexion" with "no apparent marks or scars"
3. Born free in Princess Anne County
4. Princess Anne County, August 7, 1837; Norfolk, April 2, 1855
5. January 23, 1838 and October 24, 1860

DAWLEY, JACOB

1. Born circa 1789
2. Height: 5'7"; "Black man with a very high forehead and a small scar on the back of the right hand, near his wrist."
3. Emancipated by deed of William Dawley in 1796
4. Princess Anne County [VA] October 3, 1831; Norfolk, November 30, 1832
5. July 28, 1851
6. Jacob Dawley appears in the U.S. Census of 1850 in Norfolk City. His age is given as "50" (which is surely inaccurate, since he was freed in 1796). He was described as "black" and illiterate, and he was working as laborer. He was living with Elizabeth Dawley, perhaps a daughter, age 25, "black."

DAWLEY, JAMES

1. Born circa 1820-1822
2. Height: 5'7" [in 1837] 5'5¾"[in 1845]; 5'9 and five eighths" [in 1852];"Dark complected negro boy marked very much in the face with the smallpox, with a large scar on the right cheek" [1837]; "A free negro man of black complexion, very much marked on his face and hands by smallpox, also having a scar on the left arm between the elbow and wrist" [1845 and 1852]
3. Born free in Princess Anne County; "removed to this borough to labor therein"
4. Princess Anne County, July 30, 1837; Norfolk, March 29, 1845 and April 2, 1852
5. January 23, 1838, July 28, 1851 and July 26, 1858

DAWLEY, SARAH (or "SALLY")

1. Born circa 1814
2. Height:4'11½" [1837]; 5' [1850];"light complected negro woman with a scar on her left cheek and bushy hair" [1837]; "free woman of black complexion" with "scar on the left cheek" [1850]
3. Born free in Princess Anne County; "removed to this city to labour therein"
4. Princess Anne County, August 7, 1837 and January 23, 1838; Norfolk, March 5, 1850
5. January 23, 1838 and March 1, 1855

DEMPSEY, SARAH, see SPARROW, TOM

DENNIS, PEGGY

1. Born circa 1794
2. Height: 5'1"; "Dark yellow color"; "small mole on end of nose"
3. Born free in Accomack County [VA]
4. Accomack County, April 29, 1834; Norfolk, August 27, 1835
5. July 25, 1852

_____, **DICK** [Surname not given]

1. Born circa 1827
2. 5'5 and five eights"; "Free negro man of light black complexion", "has lost sight of left eye, face slightly pitted with smallpox, scar on ball of left thumb"
3. Born free in Norfolk, proven by oath of George Rowland
4. Norfolk, August 10, 1853
5. August 2, 1858
6. "Descendant of a female Negro emancipated since first day of May, 1806"

DIGGS, LAWSON

1. Born circa 1818
2. Height: 5'2¼"; "Free man of black complexion, with scar on nose and one on bottom of left arm"
3. Born free in Isle of Wight County, "removed to this Borough to labor herein."
4. Norfolk, April 30, 1841
5. August 27, 1853

DIXON, MARIA

1. Born circa 1821
2. Height: 5'7½"; "Free woman of bright mulatto complexion, scar on upper lip near left corner of mouth, small one on forehead near edge of hair and one on underside of left arm, between elbow and wrist."
3. Emancipated in Norfolk by William M. Jackson, January 30, 1856
4. Norfolk, August 6, 1856
5. August 26, 1861

DORNEY, ROBERT FRANCIS
(Son of Mary Cornick)

1. Born circa 1836
2. Height: 4'7" [at 14]; "Negro boy of bright complexion, very difficult to distinguish from a white boy—with straight hair, two small scars on his face, one on forehead and the other under his chin—and a small scar on left hand near thumb"
3. Emancipated by will of Ann Camp, deceased, August 28, 1848

58

4. Norfolk, April 2, 1850
5. September 24, 1860
6. Dorney was enumerated in the 1860 Census in the City of Norfolk. His age was given as 23 and his color as "black" and he was working as a "boatman." He was living with his mother, Mary Cornick and her sister, Elizabeth Ruffin, and Elizabeth's three children.

DOUGLAS, CAROLINE
(Her name is spelled "Douglas" in 1846 and "Douglass" in 1850

1. Born circa 1826
2. Height: 5'4½"; "Tawny colored girl, mole on the neck and right arm."
3. Born free
4. Gloucester County, February 3, 1846; Norfolk, January 2, 1850
5. December 26, 1849 and July 26, 1858
6. "Allowed to go at large until next Court, Wm. W. Lamb, Mayor, July 21, 1858"

DREWRY, MARK

1. Circa 1817
2. Height 5'9", "A mulatto [with] scar on right hand"
3. Born free
4. Norfolk County, December 19, 1842
5. December 28, 1846

DREWRY, MATT

1. Circa 1820
2. Height 5'11", "Mulatto [with scar on left side of mouth"
3. Born free
4. Norfolk County, December 19, 1842
5. July 28, 1845

DRIGHOUSE, TULLY
1. Born August 10, 1813

2. Height: 5'8¼"; "Free man of mulatto complexion, short curly hair, small scar on back of left hand and one on upper lip, under right nostril"
3. Born free in Northampton County, "having removed from said county"
4. Norfolk, February 9, 1848
5. July 26, 1858
6. The U.S. Census of 1850 found Tully Drickus, a cook, age 35, living in the city of Norfolk with his 39 year old Sally Drickus, age 39, and 19 year old Arintha Powell. One assumes that Sally was the wife of Tully, but it was not until 1880 that the census began to identify the relationship between members of each household.

EDMUNDSON, MARTHA

1. Born circa 1814
2. Height: 5'2¾; "A free Negro woman of black complexion, with a scar on the back of the right hand, near the thumb, a small blue mole on the inside of the finger next to the little finger of the right hand, and a mole in the right eye."
3. Born free in Williamsburg
4. Norfolk City, October 2, 1846
5. February 26, 1852

_____, **EDWARD** [Surname not given]
(Son of Sally, a negro woman emancipated by Ursula [Soutigan?])

1. Born circa 1838
2. Height not taken [he was six]; "Black complexion, no apparent marks or scars"
3. Born free in Norfolk, proved by Charles B. Jordan
4. Norfolk, February 27, 1849
5. July 25, 1853

EDWARDS, AMY FRANCES
("Daughter of Belinda Edwards, free woman of color")

1. Born circa 1843
2. Height not taken [she was 7]; "Girl of black complexion" with "no apparent mark or scar on face, hands, or head."

3. Born free in Norfolk, proved by oath of Hamilton Shield
4. Norfolk, March 6, 1850
5. February 26, 1857

EDWARDS, BELINDA, see EDWARDS, AMY FRANCES, EDWARDS, LEWINIA, and EDWARDS, REBECCA

EDWARDS, LEWINIA
("Child of Belinda Edwards, free woman of color")

1. Born circa 1845
2. Height not taken [she was 5]; "Girl of black complexion" with "no apparent mark or scar"
3. Born free in Norfolk, proved by oath of Hamilton Shield
4. Norfolk, March 6, 1850
5. February 26, 1857

EDWARDS, REBECCA

1. Born circa 1848
2. Height not taken [she was two]; "Girl of black complexion" with "no apparent mark or scar"
3. Born free in Norfolk, proved by oath of Hamilton Shield
4. Norfolk, March 6, 1850
5. February 26, 1857
6. The household of Melinda (not Belinda) Edwards, as it was enumerated in Norfolk City on August 2, 1850, included:

> Melinda Edwards, 45, female, mulatto
> Mariah Johnson, 30, female, mulatto
> Samuel Edwards, 11, male, mulatto
> Amy Teamer, 7, female, black
> Lewinia Teamer, 5, female, black
> Rebecca Teamer, 3, female, black
> Margaret Hall, 13, female black

Melinda Edwards, who, like Mariah Johnson, was illiterate, owned real estate valued at $600. Neither her occupation nor that of Johnson is listed.

ELLETT, HANNAH

1. Born circa 1826
2. Height: 5'2½ [in 1846]; 5'2 and five eighths" [1853]"; "Woman of light complexion...with scar on right side of face near her mouth, from a cut" 1846]; "Woman of light black complexion with scar on right side of face, near mouth" [1853]
3. Born free in Norfolk County
4. Norfolk County, October 19, 1846; Norfolk, July 27, 1853
5. March 30, 1850 and January 24, 1859
6. "I am unable to state whether or not she is the descendant of a female slave emancipated since first day of May, 1806, except from her own representation" (Clerk, 1853)

ELLETT, LOUISA

1. Born circa 1829
2. Height: 5'; "Woman of brown complexion [with] burn just above wrist of right hand"
3. Born free
4. Nansemond County, March 11, 1850
5. March 30, 1850

ELLETT , NANCY

1. Born circa 1819
2. Height 5'5½, "Woman of brown complexion [with] no apparent marks or scars"
3. Born free

4. Nansemond County, May 10, 1841
5. December 28, 1846

ELLETT, NANCY

1. Born circa 1820
2. Height 5'1½"; "Woman of dark complexion with no apparent marks or scars"
3. Born free
4. Norfolk, September 20, 1847

5. November 24, 1851

ELLETT, SALLY

1. Born circa 1827
2. Height: 5'2¼"; "Free negro girl of black complexion" with "small scar on right cheek and small black mole near outer corner of left eye"
3. Born free in Norfolk, proved by oath of Joseph Spratley
4. Norfolk, February 3, 1846
5. July 26, 1858

ELLICK, ELIZABETH

1. Born circa 1834
2. Height: 5'1¼"; "Black complexion, scar on right side of forehead and one on third finger of right hand"
3. Born free in Surry County, as certified by "Charles Hayward, esq. a white man."
4. Surry County, September 26, 1852
5. August 23, 1858

_____, **ESTHER** [Surname not given]

1. Born circa 1788
2. Height: 5'3"; "A negro woman of bright complexion" with "scar on her forehead more than an inch long"
3. Emancipated by George Whitefield in Nansemond County on February 16, 1818
4. Norfolk, April 24, 1834

5. July 30, 1853
6. "Esther" had two children, born free in Norfolk, George, born circa 1821 and Catharine, born circa 1824

FAULK, MARTHA JANE of

1. Born circa 1832
2. Height: 5'4¾"; "Negro woman of black complexion" with "scar on the wrist of right hand near the thumb, one on her forehead, one on

her left cheek, and one on the big toe of her left foot"
3. Born free in Nansemond County, "having removed therefrom to this city to labor therein"
4. Norfolk, March 14, 1850
5. July 28, 1858
6. On September 14, 1870, the U.S. Census found Martha Faulk in Western Branch Township in Norfolk County, with a post office in Portsmouth. The household included:

> Brown, Nathaniel, 50,male, black, laborer, born Virginia
> Faulk, Martha, 35, female, black, "Works in fields"
> Faulk, James, 8, male, black
> Faulk, Thomas, 5, male, black
> Bidegood, Silvia, 80, female, black "Lives with her son"
> Bowser, Wright, 10, male, black   At home

None of the adults could read or write. It is not possible to determine, for certain, the relationships between the people in the Brown household. Mrs. Bidegood was evidently the mother of Nathaniel Brown, and one would assume that the two Faulk boys were Martha's children.

FAULK, POLLY of

1. Born circa 1824
2. Height 5'6"; "Woman of brown complexion; both little fingers deformed, cut on knuckle of middle finger of right hand, also on right side of neck and one on forehead"
3. Born free
4. Nansemond County, November 8, 1842 and September 13, 1847
5. February 25, 1850

FINNIE, CELINA

1. Born circa 1831
2. Height: 5'2½"; "Woman of light complexion" with "scar on right arm, near wrist"
3. Born free in Norfolk, proved by oath of Eliza Thomas
4. Norfolk, March 9, 1850
5. January 31, 1861

FORREST, MARY ANN SARAH
(Daughter of Julia Ann Forrest)

1. Born circa 1839
2. Height: 4'5¼:" [at age 11] "Stout made, tawney complexion, bushy hair, several small scars above left eye brow which she states were occasioned by the kick of a calf."
3. Born free in Mathews County; "removed therefrom to this city to labor therein"
4. Mathews County, March, 1850; Norfolk, April 24, 1850
5. March 30, 1850 and July 26, 1858

FOSTER, ELIZA ANN

1. Born January 21, 1821
2. Height: 5'5""; "Bright mulatto woman, compactly formed, hair inclined to be straight, small wen over left eye, which she says is disappearing, scar on under part of right wrist"
3. Born free in Mathews County
4. Mathews County, April 8, 1839
5. October 28, 1840

FOSTER, PEGGY

1. Born circa 1801
2. Height 5'1½, "Dark complexion [with] "no apparent mark or scar on head, face, or hands"
3. Born free in Norfolk County
4. Norfolk County, September 21, 1835; Norfolk, September 30, 1835

5. March 24, 1840
6. Her register states that she hd a son, John Foster

FOSTER, LOUISA

1. Born circa 1827
2. Height: 5' [1849]; 4'11½" [1851]; "A woman of light complexion, with small scar on the third joint of the little finger of the left hand and one on the thumb of the same hand, from cuts, and face marked

by small pox" [1849]; "Free woman of light black complexion" with "small scar on the first joint of little finger of her left hand, one on the last joint of the left thumb, and slight marks of smallpox about the face" [1851]
3. Born free in Norfolk County
4. Norfolk, September 17, 1849 and December 2, 1851
5. November 24, 1851 and July 26, 1858
6. "According to her own representation she is a descendant of a female Negro who was also born free" (1851)

FOSTER, MARTHA

1. Born circa 1827
2. Height: 5': "Mulatto girl, not very bright, face very much scarred by the smallpox" [1842]; "Mulatto girl of bright complexion, face much scarred by smallpox" [1850]
3. Born of free parents in Warwick County, "removed therefrom to this city to labor therein"
4. Warwick County, June 9, 1842; Norfolk, February 25, 1850
5. February 25, 1850 and July 23, 1855

FOSTER, SARAH

1. Born circa 1829
2. Height: 5'2½"; "Free negro woman of light brown complexion" with "large scar on right side of neck, caused by scrofula, and small mark or scar on nose, between eyes"
3. Born free in Norfolk, proved by oath of Elizabeth W. Ransome
4. Norfolk, August 27, 1850
5. July 26, 1858

FOULK, MARTHA JANE (of)

1. Born circa 1831
2. Height: 5'4¾"; "Black woman [with] scar on the wrist of right hand, near thumb, one on forehead, one on left cheek, and one on big toe of left foot."
3. Born free
4. Nansemond County, August 29, 1848
5. September 24, 1849

FRANCIS, WILLIAM
(Part of register is missing)
(Son of Ann Singleton)

1. Age 14
2. Height: 4' [?]
3. Born free
4. Norfolk, August 18 [?]
5. January 28, 1861
6. "William Francis has permission to pass free from arrest & is required to apply to Corporation Court [illegible] term 1861 for renewal of his register, Wm. W. Lamb, Mayor, January 10, 1861"
7. On June 25, 1880, according to the U.S. Census, William Francis, "mulatto", married, age 50, was working as a baker and living alone on Lincoln Street in the Wythe District of Hampton, in Elizabeth City County, VA.

FRAYLOR, ARCHER

1. Born circa 1814
2. Height: 5'7": "Dark brown complexion, small scar over left eye, one on right wrist, one on right arm, two or three inches above wrist, large scar on right ankle."
3. Born free
4. Petersburg, January 20, 1849
5. February 25, 1850

_____, FREDERICK [Surname not given]

1. Born circa 1828
2. Height" 5'7 and five eighths"; "Mulatto man with no apparent marks or scars"
3. Emancipated by Francis Eymeric by deed, April 26, 1850
4. Norfolk, September 1, 1851
5. July 26, 1858
6. "Permission has not been granted for him to remain in Commonwealth" (Clerk, 1858);
"Allowed to go at large till next court," Wm. W. Lamb, Mayor, July 24, 1858"

FULLER, AMY

1. Born circa 1831
2. Height: 5'"; "Negro girl of black complexion" with "scar on back of each hand and several small marks on the right cheek"
3. Born free in Norfolk, proved by oath of John Cassen
4. Norfolk, April 30, 1850
5. October 26, 1857

FULLER, BETSEY

1. Born circa 1823
2. Height: 5'2½"; "Black woman [with] small scar on left cheek and another on back of left hand"
3. Born free in Princess Anne County
4. Princess Anne County, August 4, 1845
5. April 24, 1850

FULLER, FANNY

1. Born circa 1827
2. Height: 5'6½"; "Negro woman without any apparent mark or scar"
3. Born free in Princess Anne County
4. Princess Anne County, August 7, 1848
5. February 27, 1850

FULLER, GEORGIETTA
(Daughter of Judy Fuller, free woman of color)

1. Born circa 1834
2. Height: 5'1 and seventh eighths"; "Negro girl of light complexion" with "scar on left arm between wrist and elbow and a natural mark near the right ear"
3. Born free in Norfolk, proved by oath of John Cassen
4. Norfolk, March 20, 1850
5. October 26, 1857

FULLER, HENRY
(Son of Maria Fuller)

1. Born circa 1831
2. Height: 5'5"; "Negro boy of light black complexion" with "scar on left cheek, another in corner of left eye, another on back of left hand, another on left wrist"
3. Born free in Norfolk
4. Norfolk, October4, 1836 and August 18, 1849
5. May 26, 1856
6. The U.S. Census of 1850 shows a Henry Fuller, age 21, "mulatto", living in Norfolk City on August 9, 1850 with John Fuller, age 56, "mulatto", a bricklayer who was evidently his father, and Sarah, 21, mulatto, and Thomas, 14, mulatto, who were evidently his sister and brother. Henry was a bricklayer. All but Thomas were illiterate.

FULLER, JAMES

1. Born circa 1828
2. Height: 5'3½"; "Dark complected man" with "scar on the right wrist"
3. Born free in Princess Anne County
4. Princess Anne County, August 2, 1858
5. August 5, 1858

FULLER, JUDY

1. Born circa 1811
2. Height: 5'5"; "Negro woman of black complexion" with "mark occasioned by a scald on the inside of right arm, near elbow and a scar on the forefinger of right hand, and a mole on the right cheek, and marked very much by smallpox"

3. Born free in Princess Anne County, "having removed to this Borough to labor."
4. Princess Anne County, September 7, 1835; Norfolk, September 10, 1839
5. April 23, 1838 and July 25, 1853

FULLER, MARY

1. Born circa 1827

2. Height: 5'3" [on June 24, 1850]; 5'3 and three eighths" [on July 31, 1850]; "Light complected negro woman without apparent mark or scar"
3. Born free in Princess Anne County and "removed therefrom to this city to labor therein"
4. Princess Anne County, June 24, 1850; Norfolk, July 31, 1850
5. June 30, 1850 and July 26, 1858

FULLER, MARY

1. Born circa 1830
2. Height: 4'11"; "Black woman" with "notable scar on the forefinger of right hand (the first joint of which is of")
3. Born free in Princess Anne County
4. Princess Anne County, May 22, 1854
5. November 25, 1858

FULLER, NANCY

1. Born circa 1814
2. Height: 5'2"; "Light complected negro with a small scar on the right cheek and another on the left thumb"
3. Born free in Princess Anne County
4. Princess Anne County, October 3, 1836
5. April 23, 1838
6. She was the wife of the miller, Peter Fuller.
See Fuller, Peter

FULLER, PEGGY

1. Born circa 1808
2. Height: 5'1"; "Negro woman of dark complexion, without any apparent mark or scar" [1848]; "Free negro woman of light black complexion" with "no apparent mark or scar" [1853]
3. Born free in Princess Anne County, "removed to this city to labor therein"
4. Princess Anne County, September 5, 1831 and May 24, 1848
5. Princess Anne County, July 25, 1853;Norfolk, August 13, 1853
6. Margaret Fuller, age 40, black, illiterate, was enumerated alone in Norfolk in the 1850 U.S. Census. No occupation is listed.

FULLER, PENNY

1. Born circa 1816
2. Height: 5'9" [1837]; 5'7" [1853];"Negro woman very much marked with the smallpox in the face" [1837]; "A negro woman of light black complexion", "very much marked in the face with smallpox" [1853]
3. Emancipated by deed of Sally Fuller, November 18, 1836, Princess Anne County [VA]
4. Princess Anne County, May 1, 1837 and February 10, 1840; Norfolk, August 4, 1853
5. January 27, 1840, July 25, 1853 and August 23, 1858

FULLER, PETER

1. Born circa 1807 [1840]; 1811 [1853]
2. Height: 5'11½" [1840]; 5'10 and five eights"[1853]; "Negro man of light complexion with a large scar on right leg and some smaller ones on ankle of same leg and scar on forehead" [1840]; "negro man of black complexion" [1853]
3. Born free in Princess Anne County
4. Princess Anne County, September 3, 1832; Norfolk, July 10, 1840 and June 27, 1853
5. 1853 and June 28, 1858
6. The U.S. Census of 1850 shows Peter Fuller on August 10, 1850 living in Norfolk City with his wife and children. Peter's age is given as "42". His occupation is that of a "miller." His wife, Nancy, age 31, and the couple had five children: the twins, William and Littleton, age 10; Stephen, age 7; Mary E., age 5; and John, age 2. The family is described as "black." Neither parent could read or write.

FULLER, SALLY

1. Born circa 1811
2. Height: 5'2"; "A mulatto woman" with "scar on the arm, between wrist and elbow, and a dark mark on the left cheek"
3. Born free in Princess Anne County
4. Norfolk, February 14, 1838; copy of register "accidentally destroyed or lost in removing from her house during a fire"; register

renewed February 22, 1847
5. July 25, 1853

FULLER, SALLY

1. Born August, 1833
2. Height: 5'1¼"; "No apparent mark or scar on head, face, or hands"
3. Born free in Princess Anne County [VA]
4. Princess Ann County, October 2, 1848
5. July 31, 1858
6. On July 25, 1850, Sally Fuller was enumerated in Princess Anne County, in the household of her mother, Vina Fuller, who was 50 years old, and for whom no occupation was listed. Included in the household were Charles Fuller, 20, "black", evidently Sally's older brother, and Sally, age 18, black, and Henry Fuller, a six month old mulatto boy, who seems to have been Sally's son.

FULLER, SARAH
(Daughter of Maria Fuller)

1. Born circa 1826
2. Height: 5'2½ [in 1844]; 5'3" [in 1852]; "Free woman of yellow complexion" with "no apparent mark or scar on face or hands" [both in 1844 and 1852]
3. Born free in Norfolk
4. Norfolk March 27, 1844 and August 27, 1852
5. July 31, 1852 and July 29, 1858

6. The U.S. Census of 1850 found Sarah, whose age is given as "21", living in the city of Norfolk with John Fuller, age 56, a shoemaker, who was evidently her father, and Henry, age 21, a bricklayer, who may have been her twin brother, and Thomas, age 14, who was evidently a brother. All were described as "mulatto." Of the five, only Thomas could read and write. The mother, Maria, had evidently died by that time.

GEDDINGS, LOUISA

1. Born September 14, 1830
2. Height: 5'2½"; "Color: chestnut"; "short, broad face, full eyes, thick lips, small scar directly over the backbone, just below the neck, caused by a bile [sic—i.e. boil], scar upon the left wrist from a burn, short, knotty hair"
3. Born free in Northampton County [VA]
4. Northampton County, January 10, 1848; Elizabeth City County [VA], May 3, 1849
5. April 27, 1854

GIBBONS, MARY LOUISA
(Daughter of Delila Gibbons)

1. Born circa 1837
2. Height not taken (she was eight); "Light black complexion" with "no apparent mark or scar"
3. Born free in Norfolk, on oath of N.C. Whitehead
4. Norfolk, November 14, 1845
5. July 25, 1845
6. Mary L. Gibbons, age 12, was enumerated in the city of Norfolk in the U.S. Census of 1850, in a household headed by Morris Gibson, age 27. Although no occupation is listed for him, Morris owned property valued at $200. Also in the household was Mary's mother, Delila, age 37, and Mary's sister, Sylvia F., age 14. Morris Gibbons, perhaps the uncle of Mary and Sylvia, is listed as "black"; the others as "mulatto." All of them could read and write, except for Delila.

GIBBONS, SYLVIA FRANCES
(Daughter of Delila Gibbons)

1. Born circa 1835
2. Height not taken (she was 10); "Bright complexion" with "no apparent marks or scars"
3. Born free in Norfolk, on oath of N.C. Whitehead
4. Norfolk, November 14, 1845

5. July 25, 1853
6. See Mary Louisa Gibbons

GIBSON, NANCY

1. Born circa 1830
2. Height: 5'½"; "Negro woman of brown complexion" with "no apparent mark or scar"
3. "Free born"
4. Nansemond County, October 18, 1851
5. January 28, 1861
6. The U.S. Census on August 6, 1860 for the City of Norfolk revealed a Nancy Gibson, age 25 (which would make her nine years younger than her freedom papers indicate), black, who was the wife of Oliver Gibson, 26, black. There were three children in the household: R.A Gibson., 7, male, black, John C. Gibson, 6, mulatto, and John Roy, age 10, mulatto. No occupation is given for the adults, who were unable to read or write.

GIBSON, OTWAY
("Son of Otway Gibson, a free man of color")

1. Born December 16, 1833
2. "Height is not taken in consequence of his youth" [1840]; 5'9" [at 17 in 1852]; "no apparent mark or scar on face or hands" [1840]; "free boy of dark mulatto complexion" with "scar on back of left hand and a small one on forehead, above left eyebrow"
3. Born free in Norfolk Borough, "son of Polly Gibson, a free mulatto woman whose mother was a white woman"
4. Norfolk Borough, April 23, 1838, January 12, 1840, and April 10, 1852
5. November 1, 1851 and September 27, 1858

GIBSON, POLLY

1. Born circa 1805
2. Height: 5'4½"; "A woman of mulatto complexion with no apparent mark or scar on face or hands."
3. Born free in Norfolk Borough
4. Norfolk Borough, October 9, 1835; renewed April 23, 1838,

"having satisfied the Court that the copy of her said register, formerly delivered to her, had been stolen."
5. October 27, 1851

GILMORE, AGNES

1. Born circa 1818
2. Height: 5'2½"; "Negro woman of black complexion" with "no apparent mark or scar"
3. Born free in Norfolk
4. Norfolk, March 8, 1848
5. December 26, 1860
"Allowed to apply to next Court, Wm. W. Lamb, Mayor, July 21, 1858"
On August 2, 1850, Agnes Gilmore was enumerated by the census in the city of Norfolk. Her age was given as 35, her color as "black." She had a daughter, Eliza, age 3, who was living with her.

GILMORE, MARTHA
(Daughter of Agnes Gilmore)

1. Born circa 1842
2. Height not taken; "Girl of black complexion" with "no apparent mark or scar"
3. Born free in Norfolk
4. Norfolk, March 8, 1848
5. December 26, 1860
6. On August 2, 1850, Martha Gilmore was enumerated by the census in the city of Norfolk. She was living next door to her mother and little sister Eliza. Her age is given as 15, making her considerably older than recorded in her register.

GIVENS, INDIANA
(Daughter of Sylvia Givens)

1. Born 1827-1828
2. Height: 5'1": "Yellow complexion, bushy hair, scar on the back of right hand and one over right eye" [1845]; "Woman of yellow complexion" with "scar on back of right hand and one on right eyebrow" [1848]

3. Emancipated with mother by will of William Allen, deceased, recorded January 23, 1832
4. Surry County, July 28, 1845 and October 7, 1848
5. September 25, 1848 and July 26, 1858

GIVENS, JAMES

1. Born circa 1799
2. Height: 5'7½"; "Black man [with] high forehead, short hair, stout build."
3. Freed by deed by Edmund Jones, February 24, 1840, "in consideration of the natural love and affection which he bore to his slave."
4. Surry County, February 24, 1840
5. October 8, 1848

GIVENS, JAMES
(Son of Silvia Givens)

1. Born circa 1820
2. Height: 5'2½" [1840]; 5'1" [1850]; "Small stature, round face, no scar of mark, yellow complexion" [1840]: "Free man of mulatto complexion" with "no apparent marks or scars on head, face, or hands" [1850]
3. Emancipated by will of William Allen, deceased, proved January 23, 1832
4. Surry County, February 24, 1840 and Norfolk, March 11, 1850
5. February 25, 1850 and July 26, 1858

GIVENS, MARY ELIZA

1. Born before 1824 (Her age in 1845 is given as "21+")
2. Height: 4'11¾"; "Yellow complexion, bushy hair, scar on right hand just over the thumb and one over right eye."
3. Emancipated by will of William Allen, proved in County Court of Surry, January 23, 1832
4. Surry County, July 28, 1845

5. September 25, 1848
6. Daughter of Sylvia Givens

GIVENS, MORRIS

1. Born circa 1815 or 1818
2. Height: 5'6" [1838]; 5'6½" [1845]; "Free boy of color, mulatto complexion with no apparent mark or scar" [1838] "A man of light black complexion, approximating a mulatto, with no apparent mark or scar on head, face, or hands" [1845].
3. Emancipated in Surry County by last will and testament of William Allen, deceased, "having removed from the said county to this Borough to labor therein."
4. Surry County, August 27, 1838; Norfolk, March 1, 1845
5. November 26, 1838 and July 28, 1851

GIVENS, SYLVIA (alias SYLVIA GROOMS)

1. Born circa 1832
2. Height: 5'¼"; "Yellow complexion, broad face, scar on the neck on the left side"
3. Emancipated by the will of William Allen, deceased, late of Surry County, recorded and proved in Surry County, January 23, 1832
4. Norfolk City, April 23, 1849
5. November 29, 1851

GODWIN, BENJAMIN

1. Born circa 1831
2. Height: 5'6¼"; "Man of light complexion [with] scar on right cheek and one on left hand between forefinger and thumb
3. Born free
4. Norfolk County, March 18, 1850
5. March 27, 1850
6. The U.S. Census of 1850 (August 2) shows Benjamin Godwin, a barber, 18 years old, living with William Lee, age 24, also a barber, in Norfolk Borough. Godwin was literate, but Lee could neither read nor write. While Lee was described as "mulatto", Godwin was listed as "black."

GOODRICH, NANCY

1. Born circa 1814
2. Height 5', "Negro woman of brown complexion"
3. Emancipated by last will of Mary Goodrich
4. Isle of Wight County, June 3, 1844
5. October 25, 1847

GOODRICH, VIOLET

1. Born circa 1794
2. Height 5', "Negro woman of dark complexion, scar on left eyebrow"
3. Emancipated by will of Mary Goodrich in Isle of Wight County "the date of which I am unable to ascertain" (Clerk, 1850)
4. Isle of Wight County, June 3, 1844; Norfolk, March 5, 1850
5. October 25, 1844   and July 26, 1858

GORDON, PEGGY

1. Born circa 1794
2. Height: 4'9¾"; "Free negro woman of black complexion" with "mole near corner of left eye," missing "several upper front teeth"
3. Emancipated in Norfolk by will of William D. Henley, proved June 11, 1838
4. Norfolk, July 27, 1840 and February 15, 1850
5. February 26, 1857

GRAY, CAROLINE

1. Born circa 1806
2. Height: 4'10"; "Negro woman of light complexion" with "small scar under the right jawbone"
3. Emancipated by deed of Joseph Gray, August 19, 1829
4. Norfolk, August 29, 1837
5. July 26, 1858

GRAY, CORNELIUS, see WHITE, MARY FRANCES

GRAY, HENRY

1. Born circa 1829 or 1830
2. Height: 5'9" [March, 1850]; 5'8 and seventh eights [May, 1850] ; "Man of light complexion, scar on left cheek from a burn, scar on brow of right eye from a cut, small scar on right cheek, near ear, from cut."
3. Born free in Norfolk County
4. Norfolk County, March 18, 1850; Norfolk, May 11, 1850
5. March 27, 1850 and July 26, 1858

GRAY, JAMES

1. Born circa 1835
2. Height: 5'7"; "Bright mulatto [with] no marks or scars"
3. Born free
4. Norfolk County, February 23, 1850
5. March 27, 1850
6. The U.S. Census of 1850 shows James Gray, age 15, living in Norfolk Borough, working as a "cabinet maker." He was a mulatto and was literate. He was living with Nancy Brown, age 29, mulatto, and Michael Brown, age two, mulatto. Michael was evidently Nancy's son and Nancy was perhaps James Gray's married sister. Nancy appears in the 1860 census, age 38, with her sons Mike, 11, Charles 9, and Frank 6, but James does not. James Gray may have been a brother of Henry Gray, who was registered in Norfolk at the same time, but Henry does not appear in the census.

GRAY, SALLY

1. Born circa 1831-1832
2. Height: 5'½"; "Woman of light complexion" with "scar on back of left hand near first joint of little finger, from a cut, several black moles on her face"
3. Born free in Princess Anne County, "as appears by evidence produced in court"
4. Norfolk, January 24, 1853
5. March 28, 1859

GRAYSON, MARTIN HENRY

1. Born September, 1821
2. Height: 5'6" [in 1846]; 5'7 and three eighths" [in 1851]; "Black"with a "small mole below outer corner of right eye, thick lips, dark spot on the middle of the tongue, a small scar on left hand near the root of thumb"
3. Born free in Culpeper County
4. Culpeper County, May 15, 1843; Norfolk City, July 31, 1846, "who has removed from the County aforesaid to this city to labour therein"; Norfolk City, August 4, 1851
5. July 28, 1851 and July 26, 1858
6. "Whether a descendant of a female slave emancipated since 1 day of May 1806 or not I am unable to state" (Clerk, 1851)

[GREEN], KEZIAH,

1. Born circa 1805
2. Height 5'5½", "Mulatto woman of light complexion...[with] some small flesh moles under left eye resembling black specks, long bushy hair"
3. Liberated by Watson P. Jordan by deed of emancipation, May 28, 1827, acknowledged June 6, 1827
4. Isle of Wight County, December 3, 1838
5. June 25, 1846
6. This registrant, whose surname is not given, is most likely Keziah Green, who is the only "Keziah" in the Ancestry.com index to the 1850 census whose age approximates that given in the register. She is described as 50 years old, mulatto, and a laborer with real estate valued at $200. Three children were living with her (two of whom were registered without their surnames): William Green, age 13, mulatto; Mary L. Green, age 11, mulatto; and Randal Green, age 2, mulatto.

[GREEN], MARY LOUISA or LOUISA

1. Born January 30, 1839
2. Height: 4'2½" [at 7]; 5'4¾ [at 14]; "Free Negro girl of light black complexion" with "scar on upper lip, near right corner of mouth"
3. Born free in Norfolk, proved by oath of George Rowland
4. Norfolk, June 25, 1846, August 10, 1853 and August 10, 1853
5. June 25, 1853 and January 28, 1861

6. She is the descendant of a female negro emancipated since 1ˢᵗ day of May 1806" [1853]
"Required to apply to next court for renewal of copy, Wm. W. Lamb, Mayor, January 19, 1861"

[GREEN], WILLIAM
("Son of Keziah")

1. Born October 21, 1836
2. Height: 4'8" (he was 10); "A free negro boy of light black complexion" with "scar on the right jaw, one on left cheek near the outer corner of the eye, and a large scar on the left arm, near the elbow, occasioned by a burn."
3. Born free in Norfolk, by oath of George Rowland
4. Norfolk, June 13, 1846
5. July 25, 1853

GROOMS, SYLVIA, see GIVENS, SYLVIA

GUERRAND, JUSTINE
(Daughter of Sally)

1. Born circa 1841
2. Height: 4'1½ [she was 10]; "Negro girl of mulatto complexion" with "scar on corner of right eye"
3. Born free in Norfolk of slave emancipated by John Guerrand
4. Norfolk, June 8, 1851
5. August 25, 1856

GUERRAND, MARGARET
(Daughter of Sally)

1. Born circa 1831
2. Height: 4'11½ [she was 14]; "Mulatto complexion" and "no apparent mark or scar"
3. Emancipated in Norfolk by last will and testament of John B.L. Guerrand, July 22, 1839

4. Norfolk, August 27, 1845
5. August 25, 1856

GUERRAND, SALLY

1. Born circa 1806
2. Height: 5'7½"; "Negro woman of dark brown complexion" with "scar on left side of upper lip, below the nose and another on left hand"
3. Emancipated in Norfolk by will of John B.L. Guerrand, recorded July 22, 1839
4. Norfolk, March 5, 1850
5. August 25, 1856

HALL, ALEXINA
(Daughter of Mitchell Hall)

1. Born circa 1838-1839
2. Height not taken [she was seven]; "Very bright mulatto complexion" with no apparent marks or scars on face or hands
3. Born free in Norfolk
4. Norfolk, February 16, 1846
5. 1853
6. Alexina, age 10, was enumerated in Norfolk City in the U.S. Census of 1850. She was living with Clara Hall, evidently her mother, who was 15, and like Alexina, a "mulatto." Clara owned $2000 worth of property and, like Alexina, could read and write. Also living in the household were Thomas Dunn, "black", age 70, perhaps a grandfather, and Eliza Sales, age 13, "mulatto."

HALL, WILSON

1. Born circa 1823
2. Height 5'5", "Mulatto with no apparent marks or scars"
3. Born free
4. Norfolk County, August 1, 1844
5. October 31, 1846

HAMILTON, WILLIAM

1. Born circa 1822
2. Height: 5'5¼"; "Negro man of black complexion" with "scar on left side, below breast"
3. Born free in Isle of Wight County [VA], proved by oath of N.C. Whitehead
4. Norfolk, March 4, 1850
5. April 27, 1855

HAMLIN, CHARLES

1. "Appears to be about 30" (Therefore, born circa 1819)
2. Height: 5'7"; "Black complexion, scar on left leg"
3. Born free
4. Not given
5. September 24, 1849

HAMLIN, JAMES

1. Born circa 1828, "Appears to be about 21."
2. Height: 5'8"; "Dark brown complexion, some small scars on right leg and on right wrist."
3. Born free
4. Sussex County
5. August 30, 1849
6. Hamlin appears in the 1850 Census for Norfolk. His age is given as 25, his color as "black", his occupation "laborer." With him are Sarah and Margaret Hamlin, ages 26 and 19, both "black." Margaret can read and write, but James and Sarah are illiterate.

HAMPTON, EDWARD
(Son of Nancy)

1. Born circa 1814
2. Height 5'7¼" [1845]; 5'7" [1853]: "Light complexion, scar on left cheek, just above the end of his nose, and another scar on the left hand, between the thumb and the wrist"; "bushy hair, black eyes, rather small, with white of his eyes a little yellowish" [1845]: "Free

man of yellowish complexion" with "scar on left cheek near nose, one on left hand between thumb and wrist and one between first and second joints of third finger on left hand" [1852]
3. Born free in Elizabeth City County, "son of Nancy, who was liberated by Amelia Brough of Elizabeth City County, and who "removed from said County to this city to labor therein."
4. Elizabeth City County, August 21, 1845; Norfolk, November 23, 1846 and December 8, 1853
5. July 26, 1853 and October 27, 1858

HARRIS, ELIZABETH

1. Born circa 1835
2. Height: 4'11¼"; "Light complected negro woman with a scar on the left hand, between the thumb and forefinger"
3. Born free in Princess Anne County
4. Princess Anne County, May 5, 1857
5. August 28, 1858

HARRIS, NANCY ANN

1. Born circa 1834
2. Height: 5'½"; "Bright mulatto negro woman" with "no apparent marks or scars"
3. Born free in Princess Anne County
4. Princess Anne County, April 6, 1857
5. August 28, 1858

HARRISON, JAMES

1. Born circa 1803
2. Height: 5'8½"; "Negro man of dark complexion" with "scar on inside of left thumb"
3. Born free in Norfolk County
4. Norfolk County, July 9, 1838
5. January, 1840

HARRISON, NANCY

1. Born circa 1809

2. Height: 5'4¾" [in 1850]; 5'3¾" [in 1855]; "Negro woman of dark complexion with scar on the back of right hand, near middle finger" [1850]; "Free negro woman of light black complexion" with "no apparent mark or scar on head, face, or hands"
3. Born free in Princess Anne County [VA], "removed to this city to labor herein"
4. Norfolk, March 5, 1850 and March 12, 1855
5. March 1, 1855 and October 29, 1860

HATTEN, SAMUEL

1. Born circa 1827
2. Height: 5'5"; "Mulatto man of light complexion [with] scar on left thumb"
3. "Purchased and emancipated in accordance with will of John Hatten, deceased."
4. Isle of Wight County, September 4, 1848
5. June 22, 1849

HAYES, JEMIMA VALENTINE
(Daughter of Nancy Hayes)

1. Born circa 1810
2. Height: 5'2¼; "A woman of bright mulatto complexion, having a scar on the middle joint of the third finger of the left hand."
3. Born free in Norfolk County
4. Norfolk August 3, 1840 and December 21, 1851
5. November 29, 1851 and July 26, 1858
6. "According to her own representation, she was born free in Norfolk County, the descendant of a free Negro who was born free" (Clerk, 1858)

HEARN, LAURA
(Alias Laura Johnson)

1. Born circa 1798
2. Height: 4'10"; "Dark mulatto woman" with "curly black hair" and "several front teeth decayed"
3. Born free in Mathews County
4. Norfolk, March 28, 1836

5. July 29, 1853

HENLEY, CHARLOTTE

1. Born circa 1806 [1840]; circa 1802 [1853]
2. Height: 4'10½ [1840]; 4'9¾ [1853]"; "Dark mulatto complexion" and "straight black hair",with "no apparent mark of scar on head, face, or hands" [1840]; "Dark mulatto complexion" with " small scar on left hand near first joint of thumb" and "straight hair" [1853]
3. Emancipated in Surry County by will of Bartholomew Henry, deceased
4. September 28, 1840 and August 4, 1853
5. July 25, 1853 and July 26, 1858
6. Henley had three minor children: Paulina Henley, age 11, height 4'5", of "light black complexion" with no apparent marks or scars; Indiana Henley, age 8, height not taken, "light black complexion", no marks or scars; and Elizabeth Henley, born June 2, 1835, height not taken, "black complexion" with no apparent scars

HENLEY, ELIZABETH
(Daughter of Charlotte Henley)

1. Born June 2, 1837[5]
2. Height: 4'11¼" [at 17]; "Free Negro girl of black complexion" with "no apparent marks or scars"
3. Born free in Norfolk
4. Norfolk, May 1, 1854

5. July 23, 1860
6. "Descendant of a female Negro emancipated since the first day of

---

[5] Her register in 1854 makes her two years younger than that of 1840

May 1806 (as is stated by her mother)" (Clerk, 1854)

HENLEY, INDIANA
(Daughter of Charlotte Henley)

1. Born circa 1835[6]
2. Height: 4'10 and three eighths"; "Free negro girl of dark mulatto complexion" with "no apparent marks or scars"
3. Born free in Norfolk
4. Norfolk, May 1, 1854
5. July 23, 1860
6. "Descendant of a free Negro emancipated since the first day of May 1806 (as stated by her said mother") (Clerk, 1854)

HENLEY, LOUISA
(Daughter of Charlotte Henley)

1. Born November 20, 1820
2. [1840]: Height: 5½"; "Free woman of color", "Bright mulatto complexion with straight hair" and "scar on forehead, nearly between the eyes"; [1853]: "Woman of mulatto complexion" with "small scar on forehead, nearly between the eyes"
3. Born free in Norfolk
4. Norfolk, September 28, 1840 and August 6, 1853
5. July 25, 1853 and July 27, 185
6. Henley had a son, Joseph Henley, born September 30, 1837, a boy with a "light black complexion"

HEWITT, SARAH

1. Born circa 1836
2. Height: 5'1" [at 14]; "Negro girl of light complexion" with "no apparent marks or scars"
3. Born free in Norfolk, proved by oath of Albert Smith

---

[6] Her register in 1854 makes her three years younger than that of 1840.

4. Norfolk, May 7, 1850
5. July 26, 1858

HILL, MARGARET ANN

1. Born circa 1828-1829
2. Height: 5'4¼"[in 1849]; 5'4¾" [1850]; "Negro woman of light complexion, no mark or scar"
3. Born free in Isle of Wight County, "removed therefrom to this city to labor therein"
4. Isle of Wight County, August 6, 1849; Norfolk, February 23, 1850
5. January 30, 1850 and July 26, 1858

HILL, WILLIS

1. Born circa 1833
2. Height 4'10¼ [at 23]; "Black complexion, full face"
3. Born free in Isle of Wight County [VA]
4. Norfolk, December 4, 1856
5. August 3, 1858
Hill seems to have been missed by the censuses of 1850, 1860, and 1870, but appears in Norfolk City in the Census of 1880, on June 16. By then, Hill, whose age is given as 43, was a "grocer dealer". He had a wife, Frances, age 32, and four daughters: Mary (9), Millie (5), Priscilla (3), and Rebecca (2). Also living with him was his mother, Jane, age 65. All the Hills are described as "black." Jane could neither read nor write, but the others could.

HOLLAND, AMANDA
(Daughter of Exum and Lavinia Holland)

1. Born August, 1828
2. Height 3'3¼", "Bright mulatto with no apparent scar"
3. Born free
4. Norfolk County, January 20, 1833
5. July 16, 1847

HOLLAND, BETSEY

1. Born circa 1805

2. Height: 5'4½"; "A negro woman of black complexion" with "scar on the back of her right hand and also one on the same hand near where the little finger joins the hand."
3. Born free in Isle of Wight County [VA}
4. Norfolk, August 24, 1836
5. July 25, 1853

HOLLAND, EXUM
(Son of Lavinia Holland)

1. Born circa 1817
2. Height: 5'8¼" 1844] 5'8 and five eighths" [1851]; "A free man of yellow complexion with a small scar on the forehead immediately between the eyebrows and a mole or mark on the left cheek" [1844]; "Negro man of yellow complexion with small scar on the forehead immediately between eyebrows and mole or mark on left cheek" [1851]
3. Born free in Nansemond County [VA], proved by oath of Betsey Johnson
4. Nansemond County, February 5, 1836; Norfolk Borough, July 6, 1844 and September 2, 1851
5. August 26, 1851 and July 26, 1858
Exum Holland, age 38, was enumerated in the U.S. Census of 1850, with his sister, Lucinda Holland Williams. He is described as "black", working as a "plasterer." He appears in the Third Ward of Norfolk in the 1870 census, living in the household of the sailor, Thomas Sheppard, working as a "plasterer."

HOLLAND, JUSTIN
1. Born June, 1819
2. Height 5'10¼", "Bright mulatto [with] scar on second joint of left forefinger, from a burn
3. Born free
4. Norfolk County, January 20, 1833
5. July 26, 1847
6. Son of Exum and Lavinia Holland

In 1850, Justin Holland, a "professor of music", was living as a white man in Cleveland, Ohio. He appears in the U.S. Census for the last time in 1870, still in Cleveland, as a "white" "music teacher", with property valued at $6000. He was married to Delphina, age 40, a white Louisiana native, and had three "white" daughters, Mina (16), Lavinia (13), and Clara (8). The Cleveland City directory, in which he appears for the last time in 1877-78 (which is when he must have died, in his late 50s) describes him as a Guitar Teacher.

HOLLAND, LUCINDA (Lucinda Williams in 1847)
(Daughter of Exum and Lavinia Holland)

1. Born October, 1822
2. Height 4'3¾" [at 10, in 1833]; 5'1" [1847]; 5'½" [1853] , "Bright mulatto girl [with] a very small scar across right eyebrow, from cut" [1833]; "Free woman of mulatto complexion" with "small scar across right eyebrow" [1847 and 1853]
3. Born free in Norfolk County, "having removed to this city to labor therein"
4. Norfolk County, January 20, 1833; Norfolk, August 6, 1847 and August 3, 1853
5. Norfolk, July 26, 1847, July 25, 1853, and July 26, 1858
6. "I am unable to ascertain whether or not she is the descendant of a free negro emancipated since May 1, 1806" (Clerk, 1853)
  According to the U.S. Census of 1850, Lucinda Williams was living in the city of Norfolk. Her age is given as "28". With her were the two children of her sister Nancy, Maria and John Minkins, age 10 and 7; her brother, Exum Holland, age 30, a "plasterer", and one William Rowan, age 70. Lucinda and William Rowan were "mulatto"; the rest "black." The children could read and write, the adults could not.
  She appears in the 1870 census in Norfolk with her husband, Edward Williams, who was a waiter, and her daughter, Mary, who was 17 and John, who was 26. Edward was 50 and Lucinda was 49. Lucinda was working as a waitress. All three are described as "black."

HOLLAND, NANCY (Nancy Minkins in 1847)
("Daughter of Exum [Sr] and Lavinia Holland")

1. Born December, 1823
2. Height 4'½"[at 10], "Bright mulatto with no apparent scar"
3. Born free
4. Norfolk County, January 20, 1833
5. July 26, 1847

6. Mrs. Minkins perhaps died sometime between 1847 and 1850, when her two children, Maria and John, were enumerated in the household of their aunt, Lucinda Holland Williams

HOLLOWAY, ESTHER F.

1. Born circa 1826
2. Height: 5'2"; "Mulatto woman" with scar on each wrist"
3. Born free in Isle of Wight County [VA], and "removed from said county to this city to labor therein"
4. Norfolk, August 9, 1848
5. July 26, 1853
6. The U.S. Census of 1850 records a "Hester" Holloway living in Norfolk in the household of Joseph and Sarah Butt. The Butts were white; Joseph was a "constable." Holloway is described as 26 years old and "mulatto." No occupation is listed for her. She could read and write. Also in the household was Sarah E. Holloway, undoubtedly Hester's daughter, a mulatto, aged five years.

HOLLOWAY, PHILIP

1. Born 1827
2. Height: 5'5"; "Negro man of brown complexion" with "scar on the breast, one in corner of forehead, one at end of middle finger of right hand"
3. Born free
4. Isle of Wight County, January 1, 1848
5. July 27, 1858
6. According to the U.S. Census, on August 8, 1860, "Phil" Holloway, age 31, "black" was working as a laborer and living in the city of Norfolk. He had a wife, Phillis, age 32, and four children: William (11), Susan (9), David (6), and Mary (10 months). Living with them was Jan Ricks, age 38, black, who was working as a laundress. All the adults were described as "black" and none of them could read or write.

HOLLOWAY, POLLY

1. Born circa 1821-1822
2. Height: 4'11¾"; "Mulatto woman with no mark or scar visible."
3. Born free in Isle of Wight County [VA], "removed to this city to labour therein"
4. Isle of Wight County, December 3, 1849; Norfolk, January 3, 1850
5. December 4, 1849 and July 26,1858
6. Polly Holloway was enumerated in the U.S. Census of 1850 in the City of Norfolk. Her age was given as 29, her color as "mulatto." She had two children, both listed as "black": Theophilus, 8, and William A., 2. Living with her was Martha was, 25, "black" with her son, James, 1, and Lucy Holloway, age 58, "mulatto." No occupation was listed for the women. Polly and Lucy were both illiterate.

HOLLOWELL, BETSEY

1. Born circa 1805
2. Height" 5'3½"; "Free negro woman of black complexion" with "scar on the back of her right hand and also one on the same hand near where the little finger joins the hand"
3. Born free in Isle of Wight County
4. Norfolk, July 23, 1853
5. August 23, 1858
6. "I am unable to ascertain if she is the descendant of a female Negro emancipated since 1st day of May 1806" (Clerk, 1858)

HUDGINS, IVY

1. Born circa 1821
2. Height 5'10", "Mulatto man with bushy hair and a scar on the corner of left eye"
3. Born free in Princess Anne County
4. Princess Anne County, November 7, 1842
5. November 9, 1842

HUNTER, MARY ANN
(Daughter of Nancy Bowdoin)

1. Born circa 1801
2. Height: 5'3¼"; "Mulatto woman of bright complexion" with "no

visible marks or scars"
3. Emancipated by John Bowdoin by deed, May 26, 1818
4. Norfolk, April 17, 1837
5. October 2, 1838
6. On June 27, 1870, a Virginia born mulatto Mary Hunter was living alone in Urbana, Ohio. Age 68, her real estate was valued at $600, her personal estate at $300. Under occupation, the enumerator wrote "Keeps house." She was able to read and write.

HURN, CHARLOTTE
(Daughter of Louisa Hurn)

1. Circa 1827
2. Height: 4'7" [1848]; 4'7 and one eighth [1853]; "Dark mulatto woman, stout made with scar on left jaw the size of a four pence half penny which she states arose from the toothache" [1848]; "free woman of dark mulatto complexion" with :scar on right jaw" [1853]
3. Born free in Mathews County "removed to this city"
4. Mathews County, August 12, 1848; Norfolk, August 9, 1853
5. February 25, 1850 and August 25, 1858
6. "I am unable to ascertain if she is the descendant of a female Negro emancipated since first day of May 1806" [1853]

HURN, CLARISSA FRANCES
("Daughter of Miley Hurn, a free negro")

1. Born circa 1824
2. Height 5'1", Yellow complexion, narrow scar on left check 2" long, in the direction of ear to the mouth"
3. Born free
4. Mathews County, August 8, 1845
5. November 1, 1845
6. Daughter of Miley Hurn, a free negro

HURN, MARY LOUISA
(Daughter of Charlotte Hurn)

1. Born October 20, 1847
2. Height: 3'5½ [she was five]; "small scar or mark on right cheek"
3. Born free in Norfolk, proved by oath of Anne Whitehurst

4. Norfolk, August 9, 1853

5. August 25, 1858
6. "I am unable to ascertain if she is the descendant of a female Negro emancipated since first day of May 1806"

_____JACK [Surname not recorded]

1. Born circa 1804
2. Height: 5'1½; "A negro man of black complexion, with a scar behind the left ear and another scar on the forehead"
3. "Emancipated in Norfolk County by Alice Benson, by deed recorded in Norfolk County, the date of which I am unable to state"
4. Norfolk Borough, April 24, 1837 and February 5, 1852
5. June 28, 1852 and July 26, 1858

JACKSON, HONORE

1. Born circa 1797
2. Height: 4'11"; "Negro woman of mulatto complexion" with "scar on left temple"
3. Emancipated by last will and testament of Daniel McPherson, recorded in this court (Norfolk)
4. Norfolk, February 23, 1850
5. January 28, 1861

JACKSON, SUSANNA

1. Born circa 1804
2. Height: 5'3"; "Negro woman of black complexion" with "scar on left forefinger, near hand"
3. Born free in Norfolk, proved by Henry Oatest
4. Norfolk, October 10, 1828
5. July 25, 1853

_____, JACOB [Surname not given]

1. Born circa 1812
2. Height: 5'5½"; "Negro of black complexion" with "scar between

the eyebrows, one on left cheek, near eye, one on third finger of left hand"
3. Emancipated in city of Norfolk by last will and testament of John Cooper, March 27, 1847
4. Norfolk, January 4, 1848
5. October 23, 1854

JASPER, CATHARINE

1. Born circa 1808-1809
2. Height: 5'2"; "Woman of mulatto complexion" with "scar on the right hand, between thumb and forefinger"
3. "Born of free parents" in Isle of Wight County and "resident of Borough of Norfolk" [1837]
4. Isle of Wight County, December 12, 1837 and Norfolk, May 1, 1848
5. March 27, 1838 and July 26, 1858
6. "Allowed to go at large until next Court, Wm. W. Lamb, Mayor, July 21, 1858"
Catharine Jasper was enumerated in the U.S. Census of 1850 in Norfolk City. She is described as a "mulatto", 38 years old, illiterate, with no occupation, living with John W. Jasper, age 18, "mulatto"—evidently her son—who was literate and working as a waiter.

JASPER, JOHN WALTER

1. Born circa 1834
2. Height: 5'4" [at 15]; "bright mulatto complexion", "no apparent mark or scar"
3. [?]
4. Norfolk, August 24, 1847
5. December 22, 1856
6. The U.S. Census of 1870 reveals that on August 9 of that year, in the Jefferson Ward of Portsmouth City, Virginia were living:
>John W. Jasper, 38, male, mulatto, messenger in navy yard
>Mary E. Jasper, 21, female, black
>John W. Jasper, Jr. 3, male, mulatto
>Mary E. Jasper, eight months (born September, 1869), mulatto
>George Henderson, 9, male, mulatto

Catherine Jasper, 65, female, mulatto "Lives with her son"

JASPER, WILLIAM

1. Born circa 1814
2. Height: 5'5½"; "Free negro man of black complexion with scar on the first joint of the forefinger of right hand and a mole on the nose."
3. Born free in Norfolk, proved by oaths of Lucy Dooley, Grady Locke, Samuel Doreen, and James Jackson
4. Norfolk, July 8, 1845
5. November 24, 1851

JIMMERSON, SALLY (also spelled "Jemmerson")
(Daughter of Susan Crawley)

1. Born circa 1828
2. Height: 5'1½" [in January, 1849] 4'11¾" [in October, 1849]; "Mulatto woman [with] mole on left side of neck, small scar on forehead."
3. Born of free parents in James City County, "removed therefrom to this city to labor therein"
4. James City County, January 8, 1849; Norfolk, October 2, 1849
5. January, 1849 and July 26, 1858

JOHNS, JULIA

1. Born circa 1821
2. Height 5'2¾", "Dark mulatto woman, with a mole on left side of neck"
3. Born free in Princess Anne County
4. Princess Anne County, May 1, 1843
5. December 28, 1846

JOHNSON, BARBARA

1. Born circa 1833
2. Height: 5' [register is partially illegible]; "Dark complexion"
3. Born free in Isle of Wight County
4. Isle of Wight County, April 7, 1851

5. September 27, 1858

JOHNSON, CAROLINE

1. Born circa 1835
2. Height: 5'6"' "Negro woman of black complexion" with "full face"
3. Born free in Isle of Wight County
4. Isle of Wight County, February 6, 1854
5. August 27, 1858
6. On September 5, 1850, Caroline Johnson was enumerated by the census-taker in the Eastern District of Isle of Wight County. She was living in the numerous household of Eason Goodrich, age 50, a white farmer. Miss Johnson was then 16 and listed as "F.N."—that is, "Free Negro" and "black." No occupation was given for her, but she seems to have been a servant.

JOHNSON, EDWARD

1. Born circa 1830
2. Height 4'¼"[at 12]; "Black complexion, no apparent marks"
3. Emancipated by Donald White by deed dated April 2, 1835, recorded September 26, 1842
4. Norfolk, September 26, 1842
5. August 28, 1850
6. He seems to have been the son or grandson of Lizzy Johnson, along with whom he was ordered to be registered in Norfolk

JOHNSON, FRANCES TOBIAS

1. Born circa 1813
2. Height: 5'1"[1835]; "5'¼" [1851]; "A bright mulatto woman, being marked in the face with the smallpox, having a small white scar on the left arm, a little below the elbow joint" [1835 and 1851].
3. Born free in Mathews County.
4. Norfolk, June 27, 1835; January 1, 1845; December 31, 1851
5. December 27, 1851 and July 26, 1858

6. "From her own representation, the descendant of a female Negro who was born free"

Frances Johnson appears in the U.S. Census of 1850 in the City of Norfolk, age 40, mulatto, illiterate, along with Georgiana, age 18, mulatto, evidently her daughter, and Mathew, age 2, evidently a son or grandson. Georgiana was able to read and write. No occupation is given either for Frances or Georgiana.

JOHNSON, JOE

1. Born circa 1832
2. Height: 5'8½"; "Negro boy of brown complexion" with "large scar on forehead, above left eyebrow"
3. Emancipated in city of Norfolk by will of Ann Camp, deceased, August 28, 1848
4. Norfolk, April 3, 1850
5. July 26, 1858

JOHNSON, LAURA, see HEARN, LAURA

JOHNSON, LEWIS

1. Born circa 1816-1817
2. Height: 5'9¾"; "Negro man of brown complexion [with] small scar between little finger and finger next to it on left hand"
3. "Emancipated by deed from Eliza W. Cooke, dated December 30, 1849"
4. Isle of Wight County, January 7, 1850; Norfolk, April 13, 1850
5. March 27, 1850 and March 1, 1861

JOHNSON, LIZZY

1. Born circa 1784
2. Height: 4'11¾"; "Light black complexion...middle fingers of the right hands have been stiffened by a rising; [has] lost several of her upper front teeth"

3. Emancipated by Donald White by deed dated April 2, 1835, recorded September 26, 1842
4. Norfolk Borough, September 26, 1842
5. August 28, 1850

JOHNSON, MARGARET

1. Born circa 1823
2. Height: 5'1½"; "Black woman, scar on forehead, scar on right arm, produced by burn, scar on knuckle of fourth finger of right hand and on right toe."
3. Born free
4. Nansemond County, re-registered August 10, 1848
5. August 28, 1848

JOHNSON, MILLY
(Daughter of Mary Johnson)

1. Born circa 1819
2. Height: 5'6"; "free woman of black complexion" with "scar on forehead"
3. Born free in Norfolk
4. Norfolk, February 28, 1853
5. November 25, 1858
6. "Allowed to go at large until next Court, Wm W. Lamb, Mayor, July 21, 1858" (Clerk)

JOHNSON, ROBERT

1. Born circa 1811
2. Height 5'7½" [in 1847]; 5'8" [in 1850] ; "Negro man of black complexion [with] scar under right ear" [1847]; "Negro man of dark complexion" with "scar under right ear" [1850]
3. Emancipated by deed from Eliza Clarke, Isle of Wight County, "having removed from said county of Isle of Wight to this city to labor therein"
4. Isle of Wight County, February 1, 1847; Norfolk, March 5, 1850
5. February 27, 1850 and March 3, 1860

JOHNSON, WILLIAM

1. Born circa 1821
2. Height: 5'2¼; "Negro man of light complexion" with "scar on outer end of right eyebrow, small scar on left cheek and another on back of left hand"
3. Emancipated in Norfolk City by will of Ann Camp, August 28, 1848
4. Norfolk, April 2, 1850
5. July 26, 1858

JOHNSTON, MILLY TOBIAS
(Daughter of Tobias Johnston and Fanny Johnston, "free persons of color")

1. Born September 10, 1810
2. Height: 5'4"; "Stout made, thick hair with scar on upper side of right arm above elbow, caused by puncture of a nail, short nose, thick lips"
3. Born free in Mathews County [VA]
4. Norfolk, June 5, 1838
5. July 30, 1853

JOHNSTON, THORNTON

1. Born circa 1821
2. Height: 5'2¼"; "a bright mulatto man, stout made, and has a deformity in the legs, one being longer than the other."
3. Born of free parents in Mathews County [VA]
4. Mathews County, March 10, 1851
5. March 24, 1851

JONES, ALFRED

1. Born circa 1817-1818
2. Height 5'6½"[in 1838]; 5'7¾" [in 1849], "Negro man of brown complexion [with] large scar on right hand [1838]"; "Negro man of brown complexion" with "scar on the back of the right hand, one on the right elbow joint, which has caused the joint to be somewhat stiff"; missing "two of the under front teeth"
3. Born free in Isle of Wight County, "removed to this city to labour

therein"
4. Isle of Wight County, October 1, 1838; Norfolk, September 10, 1849
5. November 28, 1846 and September 24, 1856

JONES, DAVID

1. Born circa 1816
2. Height: 5'5"; "Dark mulatto boy with scar on his breast, on his left wrist, and hand, also one on his right foot"
3. Born free in Princess Anne County [VA]
4. Princess Anne County, September 17, 1835
5. September 1, 1837
6. "George Bramble deposeth that he employed David Jones, a free colored boy, in the Borough of Norfolk to work at his kiln a short time prior or subsequent to the cholera in the year 1832. Norfolk, Virginia, Aug. 30 1837."

JONES, ELIZABETH
("Daughter of Dinah Jones, free woman of color")

1. Born circa 1832
2. Height: 5'½"; "Negro girl of black complexion" with "small scar on right thumb and another small scar on left cheek"
3. Born free in Norfolk
4. Norfolk, July 30, 1849
5. March 4, 1859

JONES, LUCY

1. Born circa 1810
2. Height 5'2½", "Negro woman of light complexion [with] scar on right wrist" [1840]; "Negro woman of black complexion" with "scar in right wrist and one on right arm, just above wrist" [1850]
3. Born free in Southampton County
4. Southampton County, September 21, 1840; Norfolk, April 1, 1850
5. November 27, 1843 and July 26, 1858

JONES, MERWIN

1. Born circa 1829
2. Height: 4'5¾"[at 14]; "Negro boy...light black complexion, no apparent mark or scar"
3. Born free in Isle of Wight County
4. Isle of Wight County, July 24, 1843
5. November 30, 1850

JONES, MISSOURI ANN
(Daughter of Lucy Jones)

1. Born circa 1838
2. Height: 4'10" [she was 12]; "negro girl of very bright mulatto complexion" with "no apparent marks or scars"
3. Born free in Norfolk
4. Norfolk, April 1, 1850
5. July 26, 1858
6. The census taker in 1850 found Missouri Jones, age 13, "black", living in the household of 39 year old, Massachusetts-born Ruth Robinson. Robinson, whose mother and daughter lived with her, evidently ran a boarding school, as the household included nine teenaged girls as well as Miss Jones and Penny and Mary Goodridge, aged 35 and 8, respectively. The Goodridges, who were "black" and Missouri Jones were evidently servants.

JONES, NANCY

1. Born circa 1814
2. Height: 5'6" [1835]; 5'5¾"; "Dark complexion with scar on the finger next to the little finger of the left hand" [1835]; "Negro woman of dark complexion" with "scar on the finger next to the little finger on the left hand and another small scar in the right eyebrow" [1850]
3. Born free in Princess Anne County, "removed therefrom to this city to labor therein"
4. Princess Anne County, September 7, 1835 and April 15, 1850
5. Princess Anne County, March 27, 1850 and July 26, 1858
6. "Daughter of Mary Jones"

JONES, PENELOPE

1. Born circa 1798

2. Height 5'1½, "Negro woman of dark complexion, no particular mark or scar"
3. Born free

4. Isle of Wight County, May 16, 1839
5. July 24, 1843

JONES, ROBERT

1. Born circa 1800
2. Height: 5'7"; "a negro man of dark mulatto complexion, nearly black" with "scar on the forehead, one on left cheek, one over left eye, and several scars on the back of the right hand"
3. Born free in Princess Anne County
4. Norfolk, July 24, 1848
5. August 23, 1853

JONES, ROBERT

1. Born circa 1825
2. Height: 6'; "Free negro man of black complexion" with "scar on the breast and one on ankle"
3. Born free in Princess Anne County, and "removed from Princess Anne County to city to labor therein"
4. Norfolk, August 13, 1847
5. July 26, 1853

JONES, SARAH

1. Born circa 1829
2. Height: 5'4"; "Woman of light complexion; three scars on back of left hand and wrist and one on back of right hand, from burns, with a blemish on the left eye."
3. Born free in Norfolk County, "removed therefrom to this city to labour therein"
4. Norfolk County, August 20, 1849; Norfolk, May 1, 1850
5. April 22, 1850 and November 25, 1856

JORDAN, HOLLAND

1. Born circa 1821
2. Height: 5'6"; "Negro woman of dark brown complexion [with] scar on top and sides of right wrist, occasioned by burns
3. Born free
4. Isle of Wight County, December 4, 1848
5. December 24, 1849

JORDAN, JOHN

1. Born circa 1832
2. Height: 5'3¼ [at 17]; "Mulatto boy" with "scar on right side of chin, another scar on the left side of neck, under the jaw, and another scar on the little finger of right hand and another scar on the thumb of left hand"
3. Born free in Norfolk, proved by oath of Charles Armistead
4. Norfolk, July 10, 1849
5. December 22, 1856
6. John Jordan and his wife and family appear in the U.S. Census for Norfolk City on August 3, 1870. Jordan, 37, male, black, was a barber. His wife, Hannah, 35, was described as "mulatto." They had eight children: Samuel, 15, Edward, 12, Eliza 9, Fannie 8, George 6, Walter 4, Mary 3, and Martha, four months (born in January, 1870). Eliza, George, and Martha were described as "mulatto", and the other children were "black." Samuel and Edward were "attending school." Their father was literate, but their mother was unable to read or write.

JORDAN, MARY ANNE

1. Born circa 1821
2. Height: 5'2¾"; "Free woman of mulatto complexion" with "scar on left side of neck just below jaw, upper front teeth decayed"
3. Emancipated in Norfolk by Moses Jordan, by deed dated May 4, 1832
4. Norfolk, September 12, 1848
5. July 26, 1858
6. On August 17, 1860, Mary A. Jordan, age 34, female, mulatto, a seamstress, illiterate, was enumerated alone. Next door, however, was the family of the barber John Jordan, 28, male, mulatto, with real estate valued at $55. Mr. Jordan had a wife, Hannah, 27, mulatto,

and four children, all mulatto: John (7), Samuel (5), Edward (4), and Harriet (1).

JOYNES, SALLY

1. "Born June, 1813."
2. Height: 5'2½"; "Bright mulatto, dark undulating hair, two upper front teeth wanting, slight scar on second joint of left forefinger, scar on back of right hand, scar from burn on right arm above wrist" [1844]: "Bright mulatto complexion, slight scar on the second joint of left forefinger, slight scar on back of right hand" [1850]
3. "Free mulatto" [1844]; "Born free in Northampton County, removed to this city to labor therein" [1850]
4. Northampton County, May 14, 1844 and February 27, 1850
5. December 26, 1848 and July 26, 1858
6. Sally Joynes appears in the U.S. Census of 1850, enumerated in Northampton County, September 5, 1850. She is in the household of John Wescoat, a bricklayer with real estate valued at $1500. With her are Peggy, William, Elizabeth, and Thomas Joynes, aged 17, 12, 8, and 7, respectively, and Mary and Elizabeth Drigges (or Driggers), age 30 and 21, respectively. All are listed as "white."

_____, **JULIA ANN** [Surname not given]

1. Born circa 1830
2. Height: 4'11" [she was 14]; "Free negro girl of light complexion with small scar on forehead over the right eye."
3. Born free in Norfolk Borough, proved by oath of Ann Gray
4. Norfolk, April 18, 1844
5. May 26, 1851

KELLAM, LEWIS

1. "Born about 1817"
2. Height: 5'3": "Light black...has lost the first joint of the thumb of the left hand"
3. "Emancipated by deed from Ann [Muir?] of record in the clerk's office of Accomack County"
4. Accomack County, August 27, 1849

5. June 24, 1850

6. The U.S. Census of 1880 shows that Lewis Kellam was living in Eastville, Northampton County, VA on June 11, 1880, along with his wife and other family members

Kellam, Lewis   mulatto 65 (head) farm laborer   illiterate
Kellam, Lovey   black 47   wife   keeps house   illiterate
Kellam, Maria   black 25 [no relationship stated] domestic servant   illiterate
Kellam, George   mulatto   8   son   Attending school
Kellam, James   mulatto   7   son
Kellam, Marion   mulatto   5   daughter
Kellam, Sarah   mulatto   1 month   daughter

One would assume that Maria was a daughter and the four children were *her* offspring.

KELLAM, MAJOR

1. Born circa 1825
2. Height: 5'5¾"; "Light yellow [with] a cut on middle finger of left hand"
3. Born free in Accomack County
4. Accomack County, March 2, 1849
5. March 26, 1849

KEMP, BILLY, see CAMP, WILLIAM

KEMP, FANNY

1. Born circa 1804
2. Height: 4'10½"; "Negro woman of black complexion" with "scar on inside of left wrist near hand"
3. Born free in Norfolk
4. Norfolk, February 15, 1850
5. July 26, 1858
6. Fanny Kemp appeared in the Fourth Ward of Norfolk in the 1880 U.S. Census, taken June 16 of that year. She was living with her son, James Kemp, mulatto, age 50, who was a barber; her daughter in law, Annie M., mulatto (47); grandson James, (23), mulatto, a laborer; granddaughter Mary, mulatto (20), who was "at home"; and granddaughter Martha, mulatto (18) who was also "at home", and

right cheek, one on first jont of the right little finger and marked in the face with smallpox"
3. Born free in Norfolk—oath of Eliza Davis

4. Norfolk, August 28, 1835 and January 28, 1850
5. July 26, 1858

LEWIS, WILLIAM

1. Born circa 1817
2. Height: 5'10½"[1848]; 5'10 and five eighths" [1853]; "A man of dark mulatto complexion, having a scar in the right eyebrow and marked in the face with smallpox" [1848]; "Free negro man of dark mulatto complexion" with "scar on right eyebrow and face very much marked by smallpox" [1853]
3. Born free in Norfolk
4. Norfolk, April 17, 1848 and September 12, 1853
5. July 25, 1853 and January 29, 1861

_____, **LOUISA** [Surname not given]

1. Born circa 1822
2. Height: 5'1"; "Free girl of mulatto complexion" with "no apparent marks or scars on head, face or hands"
3. Emancipated in Norfolk by James Murphy, by deed, January 24, 1843
4. Norfolk, February 1, 1843
5. February 27, 1858

_____, **LOUISA** [Surname not given]
(Daughter of Keziah)

See Green, Mary Louisa

LOWRAY, PATSY (or PATSEY)

1. Circa 1813 OR 1821
2. Height 5'2"[in 1838]; 5'2½" [in 1846], "Negro woman of light complexion [with] scar over left eye, and one on back of right wrist"
3. Born free in Isle of Wight County, "removed from said County to this city to labor therein"

4. Isle of Wight County, September 3, 1838; Norfolk, January 2, 1846
5. September 26, 1845 and December 22, 1856

[LUMLET], CLEMENTINE[7]

1. Born circa 1813
2. Height 5' [1842] 5' and one eighth" [1852]; "Mulatto complexion, slightly freckled in the nose, no apparent mark or scar on hands, face, or hands"
3. Emancipated by deed by William Taylor, April 26, 1841
4. Norfolk, August 11, 1842 and August 22, 1852
5. July, 1853 and July 26, 1858
6. Lumlet's freedom papers include her children: Sarah Ann, Charles Francis, and Mary Louisa, who will be listed separately under their surname "Taylor"

Clementine Lumlet is recorded in the U.S. Census of 1850 in the City of Norfolk in June, 1850.

Her color and that of her children is given as "mulatto"; her age is 45. She has five children, all with the surname of "Taylor": Sarah A., age15; Mary L., age 11, George, age 8, Clemence, age 6, and Zalae, age 2. The last three were born after the freedom papers were issued. Charles, who was between Sarah and Mary in the birth order, seems to have died between 1842 and 1850.

In 1860 census, Clementine, age 45, is using the surname "Taylor." Living with her are Mary L, age 21, Clementine, age 16, and Zeli, age 13, as well as 3 year old Mary Stokes, who may have been the daughter of Sarah, who may have married and died during the past decade. As in 1850, the entire family is described as "mulatto."

_____, **LYDIA** [Surname not given]

1. Born circa 1822

---

[7] Her freedom papers do not give a surname, which was discovered by keying in her given name and that of her children in the index to the U.S. Census of 1850 provided by *Ancestry.com.*

2. Height: 5'1"; "Negro woman of black complexion with no apparent mark or scar on head, face, or hands"
3. Emancipated in Norfolk by will of Susan Clows, recorded August 28, 1843
4. Norfolk City, August 25, 1845
5. July 26, 1852

LYONS, CHARLOTTE

1. Born circa 1811-1812
2. Height: 5'3½" [at 16]; "Negro girl of black complexion" with "no visible marks or scars"
3. Emancipated by Samuel Lyons, by deed, January 28, 1828
4. Norfolk, July 27, 1858
5. July 31, 1858
6. Charlotte Lyons was enumerated in the City of Norfolk in the census of August 6, 1860. The household in which she lived was headed by Kitty Lyons, evidently her mother, aged 88, and included a Brid Robertson "female", age 60. No occupation was listed for any of the three, and none of them could read or write.

_____, MAHALA [Surname not given]

1. Born circa 1819
2. Height: 5'2¾"; "Free negro woman of black complexion" with "small mole just above left eyebrow"
3. Emancipated in Norfolk by will of Ann Taylor, deceased, June 25, 1854
4. Norfolk, August 12, 1854
5. July 26, 1861

MARCHANT, LUKE

1. Age not stated
2. Height: 5'6½"; "Light complected negro, scar on chin and another on corner of right eye."
3. Emancipated by will of William Truss, dated July 29, 1836, Princess Anne County
4. Princess Anne County, July 6, 1846
5. December 26, 1848

_____, MARIA [Surname not given]

1. Born circa 1827
2. Height: 4'10¾"; "Black complexion, scar on right cheek"
3. Emancipated by will of Susan Clows, recorded August 28, 1843

4. Norfolk City, August 25, 1845
5. May 24, 1852

_____, MARIA
(Daughter of Bridget)

1. Born circa 1831
2. Height" 4'11½"; "Woman of black complexion" with "large cut or scar on left temple"
3. Emancipated in Norfolk by Catharine Guthrie by deed, dated August 9, 1838

4. Norfolk, April 2, 1850
5. July 28, 1858

MARLEY, SALLY

1. Born circa 1793
2. Height: 4'11"; "Dark brown complexion" with "scar over right eye, occasioned by cut and wen on right shoulder"
3. Emancipated by deed of Archibald Drew in Prince George County [VA]
4. Prince George County, July 1, 1850
5. October 30, 1858
6. "Allowed to go at large till next corporation court of this city of Norfolk, Wm. W. Lamb, Mayor, August 10, 1858"

_____, MARY
(Daughter of Sally)

1. Born circa 1818
2. Height: 4'8¾"; "Negro woman of light black complexion" with "no apparent scars or marks"
3. Emancipated in Norfolk by will of Ursula [Sautigan?]
4. Norfolk, February 27, 1844

5. July 25, 1853
6. See "Sally"

_____, **MARY FRANCES** [Surname not given]
(Child of Adele, emancipated by Ursula [Sautigan?]

1. Born circa 1839
2. Height not taken (she was five); "Light complexion, mole on forehead near right eyebrow"
3. Born free in Norfolk, proved by oath of Charles B. Jordan
4. Norfolk, February 27, 1844
5. July 25, 1853
6. See "Adele"

_____, **MARY LOUISA**, see TAYLOR, MARY LOUISA

MASON, HENRY

1. Born circa 1815
2. Height 5'8½"; "Man of light complexion [with] scar on the end of forefinger of right hand from a rising"
3. Born free in Norfolk County "removed therefrom to this city to labor therein"
4. Norfolk County, March 18, 1850
5. March 27, 1850 and July 26, 1858
6. The census of 1850 (August 26) shows that Henry Mason, age 35 (five years older than stated on his registration papers), mulatto, was working as a barber in Portsmouth, Norfolk County. He had a wife Elizabeth, a mulatto, aged 23, and a daughter Ophelia, aged 3. Henry was literate, but Elizabeth could neither read nor write.

MEARS, EMILY

1. Born circa 1825
2. Height: 5'3¼"; "negro woman with scar on left foot, caused by a burn"
3. Born free in Isle of Wight County
4. Isle of Wight County, October 7, 1850

5. November 24, 1851

MEEKS, JAMES A.

1. Born circa 1838
2. Height: 4'3"[at nine]; "Bright mulatto [with] small scar at root of forefinger of left hand, small scar on back of right hand, small scar on second joint of right little forefinger"
3. Born free
4. Orange County, September 27, 1847
5. February 28, 1850
6. James Meeks appears in the U.S. Census of 1850 for Norfolk, Virginia, age 12, "mulatto", in the household of William Meeks, 31.

MEEKS, WILLIAM
(Son of Nancy Meeks)

1. Born circa 1820
2. Height: 5'8"'; "Man of light complexion [with] scar on thumb and another on little finger of left hand, occasioned by cuts, no other mark or scar deemed worthy of notice."
3. Born free
4. Louisa County, April 13, 1846
5. August 28, 1848
6. He and James Meeks were enumerated together in the city of Norfolk on September 27, 1850.
William was described as a laborer, 31 years of age. He was a mulatto and illiterate.

MILBY, NANCY

1. Born circa 1817
2. Height: 5'4½"; "Black complexion" with "no apparent mark or scar"
3. Emancipated in Norfolk by Robert B. Stark, by deed, February 27, 1838
4. Norfolk, February 28, 1850
5. July 26, 1858
6. "She is permitted to go at large until next Court, Wm. W. Lamb, Mayor, February 21, 1858"

MILLER, NED

1. Born circa 1798
2. Height: 5'5" [1850], 5'4 and one eighth" [1855]; "Free negro man of black complexion" with "long narrow scar on right cheek, one end of it being near corner of mouth, and scar on back of left hand, near wrist"
3. Emancipated in Norfolk by deed of Aaron Milhado, December 30, 1837, admitted in court on December 27, 1841
4. Norfolk, February 4, 1850 and February 1, 1855
5. January 22, 1855 and January 28, 1861
6. Application to be made at next court for renewal of register, Wm. W. Lamb, Mayor, January 18, 1861"
   Ned Miller and his wife and children were enumerated in Norfolk City by the census on August 10, 1860:

Ned Miller, 55, male, black, caulker, real estate: $500; personal estate $200
Sally Miller, 50, female, black
Ned Miller, Jr. 22, male, black   laborer
Sally Ann Miller, 20, female, black
Clara Miller, 18, female, black
Mary F. Miller, 16, female, black
William Miller, 14, male, black
Robert Miller, 12, male, black
John Miller, 10, male, black
George Miller, 6, male, black

MILLER, ROBERT

1. Born circa 1798
2. Height: 5'7¼"; "Man of dark complexion"; "very much marked with the smallpox" with "the first joints of his little and second fingers of his left hand off"
3. Born free
4. Norfolk, September 19, 1831 and July 18, 1837
5. July 25, 1853

MINGO, ANN
(Daughter of Sally Mingo)

1. Born circa 1832
2. Height: 5'2¼"; "Mulatto girl" with "small scar on the left cheekbone and another on left arm, above wrist:
3. Born free in Norfolk City, proven by oath of Wilson Johnson
4. Norfolk, March 27, 1850
5. July 26, 1858

MINGO, SALLY

1. Born circa 1814
2. Height: 5'2½";"Negro woman of dark complexion" [1837] "free negro woman of black complexion" with "scar on right arm, just below the elbow" [1850]
3. Born in Isle of Wight County [VA] of free parents and "removed therefrom to this city to labor therein"
4. Isle of Wight County, September 4, 1837; Norfolk, March 1, 1850
5. May 28, 1840 and July 26, 1858

MINKINS, ANN MARIA
("Child of Nancy Minkins, free woman of color")

1. Born circa 1840
2. Height not taken; "Negro girl of dark mulatto complexion" with "small black mole on finger of right hand"
3. Born free in Norfolk, proved by oath of Eliza Rippon,
4. Norfolk, September 5, 1849
5. July 27, 1858
6. Maria Minkins and her brother John appear in the U.S. Census of 1850, living with their maternal aunt, Lucinda Holland Williams and her brother, their uncle, Exum Holland.

MINKINS, JOHN
("Child of Nancy Minkins, free woman of color")

1. Born circa 1844
2. "Stature not taken"; "Negro boy of light black complexion" with "small mole on nose between eyes"
3. Born free in Norfolk, proved by oath of Eliza Rippon
4. Norfolk, August 3, 1849
5. July 27, 1858

6. John Minkins, age 26, appears in the U.S. Census of 1870, living with Edward and Lucinda Williams (his aunt). He was working as a barber. His color was given as "black."

MINKINS, NANCY, see HOLLAND, NANCY

MOORE, JULIA

1. Born circa 1828
2. Height" 5'1½"; "Free negro girl of light black complexion, inclined to be yellow, having no apparent mark or scar on head or hands, but has lost one of her upper front teeth."
3. Born free as proved by oath of Fanny I. Edwards
4. Norfolk, June 27, 1842; July 19, 1847
5. 1851 or 1852
6. In August, 1850, according to the U.S. Census, Julia Moore, age 22, "black", was living in Norfolk City with 32 year old Richard Lawton, also "black", who was a sailor. She had four children: Margaret

Moore, age 7; Ansel Moore (a girl), age 5; Quarthenia, age 3; and Cornelius, age six months.

MOORE, LOUISA HENLEY

1. Born c. 1828 [1850], circa 1831 [1854]
2. Height: 5' and one eighth"; "Dark mulatto woman, stout made, with several small scars on left foot about the ankle, occasioned by scald; left eye a little crossed" [1850]; "Negro woman of dark brown complexion" with "several scars on te left foot about the ankle, occasioned by scald, left eye somewhat cross" [1854]
3. Born free in Mathews County
4. Mathews County, June 7, 1850; Norfolk, March 3, 1854
5. February 25, 1851 and February 27, 1862

MOORE, MARIA CATHARINE
(Daughter of Nancy Moore, a free woman of color)

1. Born circa 1833
2. Height: 5'1"; "Dark mulatto, stutters a little"

3. Born free in Mathews County
4. Mathews County, January 8, 1849
5. February 25, 1851

MOORE, SARAH
(Daughter of Nancy Moore)

1. Born circa 1832
2. Height: 5'3¾"; "Bright mulatto [with] black hair, two small scars on right side of face and scar on right shoulder, occasioned by burns, tolerably stout made."
3. Born free
4. Mathews County, January 10, 1848
5. September 24, 1849

MOSELEY, FANNY

1. Born circa 1828
2. Height: 4'11 and five eighths"; "Negro woman of black complexion" with "scar on the back of left hand and another scar on inside of left arm, near elbow"
3. Born free in Norfolk, proven by oath of Sylvester Dorney
4. Norfolk, August 5, 1853
5. July 31, 1858

MURPHY, JOHN

1. Born circa 1816
2. Not recorded
3. Not recorded
4. Not recorded
5. Not recorded
6. "James Murphy personally appeared in open court August 24, 1840 and declared that he is acquainted with John."

MYERS, JEREMIAH

The freedom papers of Jerry Myers contain two documents:

"New York April 12th 1838
      Your wife lately called upon me to intercede to

procure your discharge from jail. I have written to Mr. Butler the deputy keeper and have stated to him as to your being in the employ of Docr Hedges who claimed your services until you was 25 years of age and that you are now free and I have further given him a statement of what I know about you. I have also procured from the Mayor of our city a certificate of my character & which is annexed to the letter to Mr. Dutton.

If this is not sufficient for your discharge I have requested him to write to me and state what further is necessary.

I wish you to state to him any thing you may wish and he will inform me.

Jno. Lidell
20 Chambers St
New York"

"L. Dutton Esqr
Deputy Jailer

New York April 13th 1838

Sir,

A free black man named Susan called upon me to intercede for her husband, one Jerry Myers, a black who she states is in Norfolk Jail, having been shipwrecked and lost his clothes, money & she states that he is detained in jail until some evidence can be produced as to his being free and the place to which he belongs to. I know this Jerry, her husband and having been employed professionally in his behalf in Jan, 1834, after he was married in this city to this Susan his present wife. He has been in the employ of a Doctor Hedges of New Jersey, who claimed his services until he Jerry should have attained the age of twenty five years. I wrote to Doctor Hedges concerning him and received a letter from the Doctor dated January 28th 1834 of which the following is an extract "his name is Jerry or Jeremiah, he was born in Monmouth County on Friday March 1, 1811 which makes him 23 years old in March [illegible word]" "he was to serve me until he arrived at the age of 25 years" Doctor Hedges then purposed to relinquish his claim to Jerry's services for the sum of seventy five Dollars of which sum I paid some $9 or 10 on account. After this I met Jerry in the streets at intervals frequently for upwards of a year and know of his being at service here for some months and presumed that he had arranged with the Doctor for his time.

Being upwards of 25 years of age of this time he is now his own master and must be considered a <u>free man</u>. My best recollection of his size and appearance is as following—viz. In height, from 5 ft 6 to five ft 7 inches thereabouts—Complexion rather light for a Negro. I would not call him exactly a Mulatto but he is not so dark as Negroes generally. He has a good face, intelligent and good natured. I recollect no particular marks upon his person with which to distinguish him. His wife is a smart, active, and industrious woman of excellent character and is greatly afflicted at her husband's situation and misfortune. She was at service in my father's family upwards of 15 yars since & I have been thus particular that you may be satisfied as to the fact of Jerry being free and a person of good character and in hopes that he may be liberated and return to this city, his home, as soon as practicable.

Should any evidence further than my statement be necessary, when being informed I will transmit the same. I can assure you that there is no manner of doubt of his being born and brought up in New Jersey, and of his being free and also of his being a married man and a resident of this city.
Respectfully
Your [illegible word]
John A. Lidell
Counselor at Law
No. 20 Chambers St
New York City"

Also enclosed was this note:

Mayor's Office
New York, April 17th 1838
I, Aaron Clark, Mayor of the City of New York, Do hereby certify that I am well acquainted with John A. Lidell, Esquire, the writer of the within Letter, that he is a Counsellor at Law of respectability and standing in this City and that full faith and credit are due to the statement by him therein made.
Given under my hand the day and year above written,
Aaron Clark,
        Mayor

Myers' freedom papers contain only the words "1838, Apl.

23d to be discharged"

_____, NANCY [Surname not given]

1. Born circa 1823
2. Height: 5'4"; "black complexion" with "scar on left arm, above wrist"
3. Born free in Norfolk
4. Norfolk, April 1, 1837 and February 23, 1850
5. July 26, 1858

NEWBY, BARTHENA

1. Born circa 1824
2. Height: 5'3½"; "Negro woman of dark complexion"
3. Born free in Isle of Wight County
4. Isle of Wight, June 1, 1857
5. July 31, 1858

NEWSOM, BETTY

1. Born circa 1807
2. Height: 5'½"; "Negro woman of black complexion" with "scar near outer corner of left eye, near temple"
3. Emancipated in Norfolk by Mary Chandler, by deed, dated January 18, 1836
4. Norfolk, September 20, 1838
5. July 26, 1853
6. Newsom had two sons: Daniel, "a boy of black complexion", aged "about 7" [born circa 1831], and William, "a boy of black complexion", aged "about 3 years and six months" [born circa March, 1835]

OGILVIE, MARY

1. Born circa 1812
2. Height: 5'¾"; "Girl of light complexion [with] mole on back part of neck and under left ear"
3. Born free
4. Norfolk Borough, September 24, 1834
5. August 26, 1850

OWENS, CYNTHIA ("ALIAS SUKEY OWENS")

1. Circa 1811
2. Height 5'3" [1846]; 5'2 ¾" [1853], "Negro woman of dark complexion with scar on left cheek, near corner of mouth" [1846]: "Woman of black complexion" with " scar on left cheek, near corner of mouth" [1853]
3. Emancipated in Norfolk County by will of John Owens, dated July 16, 1818
4. Norfolk County, September 21, 1846; Norfolk, November 4, 1846 and August 4, 1853
5. October 30, 1846, July 25, 1853, September 27, 1858
6. "Permission has not been granted her to remain in the state by this court" (Clerk, 1858)

OWENS, MARY ANN

1. Born circa 1830 or 1832
2. Height: 5'1¼"[April, 1850]; 5'1¾ [November, 1850]; "Woman of light complexion [with] small scar below right cheekbone from a burn, and a scar on the little finger from a cut" [April, 1850]; 'woman of light black complexion" with "small scar on right cheek occasioned from a burn, one on right little finger, caused by cut, and small one on side of left wrist" [November, 1850]
3. Born free in Norfolk County, "removed from County of Norfolk to this city to labour therein"
4. Norfolk County, April 15, 1850; Norfolk, November 7, 1850
5. April 22, 1850 and August 25, 1856
6. "Descendant of a female Negro emancipated since the 1st day of May 1806"

OWENS, ROSE

1. Born circa 1812
2. Height: 5'3½"; "A woman of dark complexion" with "scar on lower joint of left thumb, from a cut."
3. Emancipated by will of John Owens, dated July 16, 1818
4. Norfolk County, October 26, 1846
5. July 30, 1853

PAGE (OR PAIGE), JUDITH (FORMERLY JUDITH RILIE)

1. Born circa 1815
2. Height 4'11¾ [1838]; 5'½" [1852]:, "Mulatto woman [with] scar on right arm, near elbow"
3. Born free in Gloucester County, "removed to this city to labor herein"
4. Registered in Williamsburg, VA May 20, 1838; Norfolk, March 3, 1847 AND September 10, 1852
5. August 23,1852 and February 28, 1859
"Judith is allowed to pass with these papers till next term of the Corporation Court, when she is to apply for the renewal of them, Feb 3, 1859, Wm W Lamb, Mayor"

PAGE, SALLY
(Daughter of Judith Page)

1. Born circa 1821
2. Height: 5'½"; "Tawney complected girl [with] scar on right arm, one on the left arm, just above wrist, and one between her eyebrows"
3. Born free in Williamsburg
4. Williamsburg, January 1, 1849
5. January 22, 1849

PARROTT , ELIZA JANE
(Child of Louisa Parrott)

1. Born circa 1839
2. Height: 4'7"; "Negro girl of black complexion" with "no apparent scar on head, face, or hands"
3. Born free in Mathews County
4. Norfolk, September 23, 1851
5. July 27, 1858
6. "I am unable to state whether or not she is a descendant of a female slave emancipated since the first day of May 1806" (clerk)

PARROTT, SARAH

1. Born circa 1809

2. Height: 5'7¾"; "Free born mulatto woman"; "spare form small scar on right thumb, one on right, occasioned by burn"
3. Born free in Mathews County
4. Mathews County, December 5, 1834
5. June 29, 1838

PARROTT, SARAH FRANCES
(Child of Louisa Parrot) [1838] (Child of Louisa Parrott, deceased) [1851]

1. Born 1836 [1838]; 1835 [1851]
2. [1838] "Height not taken, being too young"; "A negro girl of light black complexion"; [1851] height: 5'; "Negro girl of light black complexion" with "several scars on or about right wrist"
3. Born free in Mathews County
4. Norfolk, June 21, 1838 and September 23, 1851
5. August 26, 1851
6. "I am unable to state whether or not she is a descendant of a female slave emancipated since the first day of May, 1806" (Clerk)

PARSONS, JOE

1. Born circa 1809
2. Height 5'6", "Mulatto man with a scar on the right hand and joint of the forefinger with bushy hair"
3. Born free in Princess Anne County
4. Princess Anne County, August 7, 1837
5. July 26, 1847

PATTERSON, MARY (ALIAS MARY RUFFIN), see RUFFIN, MARY

PAYNE, CHARLOTTE

1. Born circa 1823
2. Height: 5'5"; "Free woman of bright mulatto complexion", "no apparent mark or scar on head, face, or hands"

3. Born free in Norfolk, proved by oath of William Winston
4. Norfolk, October 31, 1854
5. January 28, 1861
6. "I am unable to ascertain whether or not she is the descendant of a female negro emancipated since 1st day of May 1806" [1854]

PERKINS, JOHN

1. Born circa 1808
2. Height: 5'8¼"; "Free man of color, of yellow complexion" with "mark or scar on his right eyebrow, occasioned by a cut; also in left eyebrow"
3. Born free in Nansemond County
4. Norfolk, April 5, 1837
5. July 25, 1853
6. John Perkins, age 50, a ship's carpenter, was enumerated in the U.S. Census of 1850 in Norfolk City, along with his wife, Cecelia, age 49, and Grace Gardner (perhaps his mother-in-law), age 80.
All were described as "mulatto." Of the three, only Cecelia could read and write.

PERRY, BETSEY, see PERRY, MARY LOUISA

PERRY, MARY LOUISA
(Daughter of Betsey Perry)

1. Born circa 1839
2. Height" 4'10" [at 14]; "Free Negro girl of black complexion" with "two large scars on right arm, one above and the other below elbow"
3. Born free in Norfolk, proven by oath of Charles G. Armistead
4. Norfolk, August 9, 1853
5. October 29, 1858
6. "Descendant of a free female Negro emancipated since 1st day of May 1806"

PEYTON, NANCY ("ALIAS NANCY HYATT")

1. Born circa 1825
2. Height: 5'5¼"; "Dark complexion, scar on left arm and wrist."
3. Born free
4. Mathews County, August 8, 1845

5. August 28, 1845

6. "Daughter of Jane Hyatt". The U.S. Census reveals a Nancy Payton [sic], age 25, black, with no occupation stated, living in the City of Norfolk on August 7, 1850, with Brister Rudd, who was ordered to be registered in Norfolk two years earlier.

PIERCE, ELIZA

1. Born circa 1826 or 1827

2. Height: 5'4½"[in February, 1848] 5'3½ [in September, 1848]; "Woman of brown complexion [with] scar on knuckle of the thumb, one on the knuckle of forefinger of the left hand and a mole on left side of neck" [in February, 1848]; "Negro woman of light black complexion" with "scar on the knuckle of the left hand, one on the knuckle of the forefinger of her left hand, and a mole on the left side of the neck" [September, 1848]

3. Born free in Nansemond County

4. Nansemond County, registration renewed, February 14, 1848; Norfolk, September 4, 1848

5. August 28, 1848 and July 26, 1858

PIERCE, HARRISON of

1. Born circa 1831

2. Height: 5'6 and seven eighths"; "Free man of black complexion" with "scar on right wrist and one on the back of his right hand"

3. Born free in Nansemond County

4. Nansemond County, January 13, 1852

5. April 24, 1860

PIERCE, JACOB (of)

1. Born circa 1830

2. Height: 5'7½"; "Man of black complexion [with] scar on the forefinger of left hand

3. Born free

4. Nansemond County, August 5, 1847

5. March 30, 1850

PIERCE, WILLIAM (of)

1. Born June, 1806
2. Height: 5'9½" [1847]; "5'8" [1849]; "Black man [with] several scars, one on left thumb nail, one on right hand, one on right large toe, and one just above the ankle on right leg" [1847]; "Negro man of black complexion" with "scar at end of left thumb, scar on right hand between thumb and forefinger, one other scar on right large toe and one other scar on ankle of left leg" [1849]
3. Born free in Nansemond County and "removed therefrom to this city to labor therein"
4. Nansemond County, registry renewed August 9, 1847; Norfolk, September 4, 1849
5. July 23, 1849 and August 24, 1858

PIERCE, WILLIAM (of)

1. Born circa 1829
2. Height" 5'5½"; "Man of brown complexion [with] scar over left eye and one on right arm"
3. Born free
4. Nansemond County, March 28, 1850
5. March 30, 1850

PINNS, BETSEY

1. Born circa 1820
2. Height: 5'6"; "Free woman of very bright mulatto complexion" with "scar on the under part of left jaw"
3. Born free in Norfolk
4. Norfolk, October 11, 1852
5. July 27, 1858

PITTS, CALEB

1. "Born in or about Christmas 1807"
2. Height: 5'4" [1833]; 5'4¾" [1850]; and one tenth"; "Mulatto [with] black bushy head, prominent forehead, scar across left eyebrow, small, dark mole near right side of nose, broad nose, thick, protruding lips, mole on left arm on inside, above elbow" [1833]; "Negro man of mulatto complexion" with "scar across left eyebrow, small dark mole near left side of nose and mole on left arm in inside, above elbow"

[1850]
3. "Emancipated... by the will of John Pitts, recorded in Northampton County Court, March 8, 1819."
4. Northampton County, April 8, 1833; Norfolk, February 4, 1850
5. January 30, 1850 and July 31, 1858
6. On June 19, 1860, Caleb Pitts and family were enumerated by the U.S. Census in the City of Norfolk. Caleb, age 55, "mulatto", was a drayman. In his household were:
> Tamer Pitts [evidently his wife], age 35, female, black
> W. Pitts, age 12, male, black
> C Pitts, age 12, male, black
> Will Pitts, age 7, male, black
> James Pitts, age 5, male black

POLLARD, SALLY

1. Born circa 1810
2. Height: 4'9¾"; "Woman of mulatto complexion, marked on face with smallpox"
3. Born free in Norfolk, proven by oath of William W. Sharp
4. Norfolk, April 3, 1850
5. March 24, 1858

POOL, SALLY

1. Born December 20, 1829
2. Height: 4"11 and seven tenths of an inch; "Bright mulatto with round full face, straight black hair, short blunt nose, small scars in forehead and over left eye and under left cheek, scar on forefinger of left hand and wart on fleshy part of back of right hand"
3. Born free in Northampton County
4. Northampton County, June 14, 1847
5. February 25, 1850

PORTER, POLLY (of)

1. Born circa 1814
2. Height 5'2¾", "Black woman [with] small scar over right eye and two scars on right arm between elbow and hand"
3. Born free
4. Nansemond County, September 10, 1838

5. October 27, 1849

PORTER, SALLY

1. [Register is deteriorated; age not legible]
2. [Height not legible]: "Black complexion," "scar over right eye"
3. Born free
4. Norfolk, April [?].1850
5. July 23, 1850

PORTER, WASHINGTON (of)

1, Born circa 1797
2. Height: 5'5¾:; "Man of black complexion with a scar on the joint of the elbow of right arm, occasioned by a burn and his little finger on right hand crooked"
3. Born free
4. Norfolk, September 14, 1831
5. September 22, 1851
6. Washington Porter, "black", age 50, is enumerated in the 1850 Census of Norfolk City, along with his wife, Eliza, age 40 "black", and Elizabeth Oden, age 19, "black." None of the three could read or write.

PORTLOCK, CELINA

1. Born circa 1808
2. Height: 5'3" "Negro woman of black complexion" with "no apparent mark or scar"
3. Born free in Norfolk County, proved by oath of John Palmer
4. Norfolk, March 11, 1850
5. July 26, 1858
The U.S. Census of 1850, taken in August in the City of Norfolk, shows the following family:
     Lucy Portlock, 36, female, black
     Sarah Portlock, 37, female, black
     Celina Portlock, 42, female, black
     Mary Portlock, 17, female, mulatto
     Anthony Portlock, 12, male, mulatto
Mary and Anthony could read and write. One would assume that Lucy, Sarah, and Celina were sisters, and that Mary and Anthony

were the children of one of the three.

The U.S. Census of 1860 (July 13,) reveals the following household in the City of Norfolk:

> Sarah Portlock, 47, female, black, laundress, illiterate
> Eliza Portlock, 50, female, black, laundress, illiterate
> M.A. Banks 27, female, mulatto, laundress, illiterate
> Lucy Portlock, 43, female, black, laundress, illiterate
> Anthony Banks, 23, male, black [no occupation given], illiterate

The three Portlock women were evidently sisters. Could "Eliza" had been the same person as "Celina"? Mary and Anthony were now known as Banks, rather than Portlock.

Celina was living with Anthony Portlock and Mary Banks in 1880, which would lead one to believe that Anthony and Mary were her children. According to the U.S. Census of the city of Norfolk, living in the Third Ward on July 28, 1870 were:

> Portlock, Anthony., 32, male, mulatto, shoemaker
> Portlock, Lucy, age 30, female, mulatto, "wash and iron"
> Portlock, Louis 10, male, mulatto
> Portlock, Anthony, 8, male, mulato
> Portlock, Mary 3, female, mulatto
> Portlock, Ann 3, female, mulatto, 6 mos.
> Portlock, Selina, 70, female, black

Celina Portlock must have died between 1870 and 1880. Son Anthony, during that interval, lost his wife Lucy, because in the census of 1880, still living in Norfolk city, he is married to 25 year old Mary, and has by her Robert, 5, and Selina, 3, who seems to be named for his late mother.

PORTLOCK, SARAH
(Daughter of Polly Portlock)

1. Born circa 1813
2. Height: 5'; "Free negro woman of light black complexion" with "no apparent mark or scar"
3. Born free in Norfolk, proven by oath of James Murphy
4. Norfolk, January 30, 1850 and March 28, 1855
5. February 28, 1855and March 26, 1860

POWELL, ELIZABETH

RANN, ISAAC

1. Born circa 1806
2. "Brown complexion, scar in left eyebrow, one below right eye, one on forehead near left temple, two fingers of right hand are crooked (first and second), large scar on right arm above elbow."
3. Born free
4. Petersburg, August 21, 1849
5. September 24, 1849

READ, EMMELINE

1. Born circa 1828
2. Height: 5'3"; "Woman of brown complexion [with] scar on left cheek and one over right eye"
3. Born free
4. Nansemond County, January 14, 1850
5. February 27, 1850

READ, JOHN of

1. Born circa 1810
2. Height: 5'1¼"; "Negro man of black complexion" with "scar in palm of left hand"
3. Born free in Nansemond County [VA]
4. Norfolk, May 2, 1850
5. May 24, 1858

REDDICK, JACOB

1. Born circa 1810
2. Height: 5'6¼"; "Free negro man of black complexion" with "scar between the eyebrows and one on left cheek, one on third finger of the left hand, and wen on left wrist"
3. Emancipated in Norfolk by last will and testament of John Cooper, March 27, 1847
4. Norfolk, October 23, 1854
5. January 28, 1861
"Application to be made for renewal at Jan term 1861 of Corporation

Court, Wm. W. Lamb, Mayor"
Reddick was living on August 11, 1870, according to the U.S. Census, in the Second Ward of the City of Norfolk, and working as a barber.

Reddick, Jacob, 53, male, black, barber, born Virginia
Reddick, Sarah, 36, female, mulatto, "keeping house", born Virginia
Reddick, Maria, 17, female, mulatto, school teacher, born Virginia
Reddick, John, 14, male, mulatto, Attending school, born Virginia
Reddick, Nancy, 9, female, mulatto, born Virginia
Reddick, Sarah, 7, female, mulatto, born Virginia
Reddick, Jacob, 5, female, mulatto, born Virginia
All the adults could read and write

REID, JAMES

1. Born circa 1822
2. Height: 5'5"; "Brown complexion, mole on right side of nose and two on outer corner of right eye, scar on right side of neck."
3. Born free
4. Petersburg, February 28, 1848
5. July 29, 1848

_____, **REUBEN** [Surname not given]
(Son of Celia)

1. Born circa 1842
2. Height: 4'3" [at 8]; "Negro boy of black complexion" with "no apparent marks or scars on face, head, or hands"
3. Born free in Norfolk—proved by Reuben H. Clarke
4. Norfolk, March 6, 1850
5. July 26, 1858

_____, **REUBEN**
("Son of Lydia, free woman of color")

1. Born circa 1847
2. Height not taken [he was three]; "Boy of bright mulatto complexion" with "scar near right side of forehead"
3. Born free in Norfolk, proved by oath of Sylvester Dorney

4. Norfolk, March 4, 1850
5. March 3, 1859

RICKS, CELIA ANN

1. Born circa 1824
2. "Black woman, no scars on head or hands; scar on left cheek near eye"
3. Born free in Southampton County, "removed therefrom to this city to labour therein."
4. Southampton County, August 17, 1844
5. December 27, 1847 and again on July 25, 1853

RICKS, ELIZA

1. Born circa 1813
2. Height 5'4", "Negro woman of black complexion with scar on left wrist and one on left side of the forehead"
3. Born free in Southampton County, "removed therefrom to this city to labor therein"
4. Southampton County, June 17, 1844; Norfolk, February 18, 1845
5. October 18, 1844   and July 26, 1858

RICKS, EMMA JANE
("ALIAS EMMA JANE CAMP, DAUGHTER OF ADALINE SPARROW")

1. Born circa 1835
2. Height: 5'1"; "woman of light complexion" with "no apparent mark or scar"
3. Born free in Norfolk County
4. Norfolk County, June 29, 1852
5. June 22, 1857
See Camp, William

RICKS, JENNY

1. Born circa 1814
2. Height 5'¾", "Negro woman of black complexion [with] scar on right arm"
3. Born free in Southampton County

4. Southampton County, June 17, 1844
5. October 28, 1844

RICKS, MARTHA

1. Born circa 1835
2. Height: 4'11½"; "Brown complexion" with "no marks or scars on head, face, or hands"
3. Born free in Southampton County
4. Southampton County, April22, 1856
6. July 31,1858

RICKS, MONROE MADISON

1. Born circa 1809
2. Height: 5'4½"; "Free man of light complexion; scar near the middle joint of right forefinger, one on the first joint of the left forefinger, and one on the under lip"
3. Apparently born free
4. Southampton County, September 17, 1831; Norfolk Borough January 10, 1834
5. July 25, 1853
6. In 1850 Monroe Ricks, age 45, was enumerated with his wife Ailsey, who was the same age. Both were described as "black" and illiterate. Monroe was working as a cook.

RICKS, POLLY

1. Born circa 1827
2. Height: 5'4½"; "Negro woman of dark complexion, scar on right cheek."
3. Born free
4. Isle of Wight County, October 2, 1848
5. August 28, 1849
6. Polly Ricks was enumerated in the "City of Norfolk" on August 15, 1850. She was 20 years old, "black," illiterate. She had a daughter Ann E, aged 3, "black". Ricks was the head of a household that included Mary Wilson, 21, black, and Margaret Roberts, 21, Jane Roberts, 18, Victoria Roberts, 10, and James R. Roberts 7—all "black." There is no occupation listed for any of the adults.

RICKS, RICHARD, see BURROWS, DICK

RICKS, ROBERT

1. Born circa 1810
2. Height: 5'6"; "Negro man of light complexion" with "small scar on the forefinger of left hand"
3. Born free in Southampton County
4. Southampton County, September 19, 1836
5. February 26, 1838

6. This is probably the same Robert Ricks who was enumerated by the U.S. census August 2, 1850 in Norfolk. His color was given as "black" and his age was given as 30 (which would have made him a decade younger than his register stated that he was. He was working as a stevedore and had a wife, Jane, 28, black, and a daughter, Martha, 11, black.

ROBERTSON, JORDAN

1. Born circa 1818
2. Height: 5'2¾; "Negro man of black complexion with scar on the back of left wrist, two small ones on the right cheek and one near the right temple"
3. Born free in Nansemond County, proved by oath of Robert Jones, Jr.
4. Norfolk City, July 27, 1840
5. December 28, 1852
6. Jordan Robertson and his wife Nancy were enumerated in the U.S. Census of 1850 in the City of Norfolk, along with their four children. The age of both Jordan and Nancy was given as "26". Jordan was a "drayman." The children were: Patsy A., age 7; Louisa, age 6; Sarah E., age 3; and Milly, age 1. Neither parent could read or write and all members of the family were described as "black."

ROBERTSON, NANCY [TYNES]
(Daughter of Patsy Godwin)

1. Born circa 1823
2. Height: 4'11¼"; "Light black complexion, with no apparent marks

or scars on head, face, or hands"
3. Born free in Norfolk, proved by oath of Eliza Thomas
4. Norfolk, October 24, 1842 and January 8, 1853
5. December 28, 1852
6. "I am unable to state whether she is a descendant of a female negro emancipated since the first day of May 1806".
Wife of Jordan Robertson, Nancy was living in the same neighborhood as her sister, Minerva Tynes Camp and her children.

ROBINSON, CHARLES EDWARD
(Son of Margaret Ann Robinson)

1. Born circa 1837
2. Height: 4'6 and one eights" [he was 14]; "Free negro boy of black complexion" with "small scar in the nose, just between the eyes"
3. Born free in Norfolk County
4. Norfolk, December 2, 1851
5. July 26, 1853
6. "According to the representation of his mother, he is the descendant of a female Negresses in the maternal line who were born free as far back as his great-grandmother." (Clerk)

ROBINSON, EMMA ELIZABETH
(Daughter of Margaret Ann Robinson)

1. Born circa 1838
2. Height : 4'5½" [at 13]; "Free negro girl of light black complexion" with "scar on right wrist, occasioned by a burn"
3. Born free in Norfolk County, proven by oath of Richard B. Wright
4. Norfolk, December 2, 1851
5. July 26, 1858
6. "According to the representation of her mother, she is a descendant of a female Negress in the maternal line who was born free as far back as her grandmother[8]" (Clerk)

---

[8] Charles and Emma Robinson were brother and sister, yet, according to Clerk John Williams, Emma was descended from free Negro women as far back as her "grandmother" and Charles was descended from free Negro

ROBINSON, JAMES HENRY of

1. Born circa 1828
2. Height: "5'4¾"; "Light complexion, no apparent mark or scar [January 8, 1849]; "Free Negro man of light black complexion" with "no apparent mark or scar" [1849 and 1854]
3. Born free in Nansemond County

4. Nansemond County, January 8, 1849; Norfolk, January 31, 1849 and February 9, 1854
5. January 22, 1849, January 23, 1854 and February 28, 1859

ROBINSON, JOHN WILLIAM

1. Born circa 1826
2. Height: 5'6¾"; "Man of brown complexion [with] no apparent mark or scar
3. Born free
4. Nansemond County, December 10, 1847
5. December 26, 1849

ROBINSON, MARGARET ANN

1. Born circa 1817
2. Height: 5': "Woman of brown complexion, no apparent scar."
3. Born free
4. Nansemond County, November 8, 1847
5. March 3, 1849
6. "Margaret A. Robinson" was enumerated in the "City of Norfolk" September 27, 1850. Her age was listed as 34, her color as "black."

---

women as far back as his "great-grandmother." Obviously there was an error on the part of the clerk.

She was illiterate, with no occupation. She had two children, both "black," Charles E., 13 and Emma E. 11, both of whom could read and write.

ROBINSON, MARY ANN

1, Born circa 1817
2. Height: 5'; "Woman of brown complexion" with "no apparent mark or scar"
3. Born free in Nansemond County, and "removed therefrom to this city to labor therein"
4. Norfolk, March 8, 1849
5. July 26, 1858
6. Mary Ann Robinson is doubtless the same person as Margaret Ann Robinson (above)

RODNEY, WILLIAM ALFRED

1. Born circa 1829
2. Height 5'6_", "Tawney complexion, no mark or scar"
3. Born free
4. King and Queen County, January 14, 1850
5. February 25, 1850

ROGERS, ARENA

1. Born circa 1804
2. Height: 5'2"; "Black"; "small scar on the joint of left thumb"
3. Born free in Accomack County [VA]

4. Norfolk, August 31, 1835
5. September 26, 1853

RONY, MARY CATHARINE

1. Born circa 1813
2. Height: 5'½"; "Free mulatto woman" with scar on left arm, above elbow"
3. Born free in King and Queen County
4. Norfolk, February 18, 1850
5. July 26, 1858

6. "Allowed to go at large till next court, Wm. W. Lamb, Mayor, July 20, 1858"

_____, **ROSE** [Surname not given]

1. Born circa 1796
2. Height: 5'1and one eighth"; "Negro woman of black complexion" with "scar on forehead"
3. Emancipated in Norfolk by Eunice Reed, executrix of Henry Reed, deceased, by deed, dated September 18, 1850
4. Norfolk, September 30, 1850
5. July 26, 1858

ROSS, MARTHA ANN

1. Born circa 1829
2. Height: 4'11"; "Mulatto woman" with "small scar on inner part of left wrist"
3. Born free
4. Nansemond County, January 29, 1850 and Norfolk, March 26, 1850
5. February 11, 1850 (Nansemond County) and May 3, 1855

ROSS, NANCY, see ARMISTEAD, GEORGIANNA

ROYSTON, WILLIAM
(Son of Fanny Royston)

1. Born circa 1818
2. Height: 5'2"; "Free born mulatto man, stout made, bushy hair, thick lips, sound teeth, scar about big toe of left foot"
3. Born free in Mathews County

4. Mathews County, May 12, 1838
5. July 30, 1853

RUDD, BRISTER

1. Born circa 1803
2. Height: 5'8½" "in shoes"; "Short hair, small knot on left temple near top of ear and scar from the cut of a knife on the right thumb,

small scar apparently from a burn between first and second joints of little finger of left hand."

3. Emancipated by George Hope, "duly recorded" August 29, 1846
4. Elizabeth City County, May 25, 1848
5. June 26, 1848
6. The Census of 1850 enumerates a Brister Rudd, age 49, black, a whitewasher, living in the City of Norfolk on August 7, with Nancy Payton.

RUFFIN, ELIZABETH

1. Born circa 1822
2. Height: 4'9¼"; "Negro woman of black complexion" with "large scar on her left arm above wrist"
3. Emancipated by Ann Camp, deceased, August 28, 1848
4. Norfolk, November 20, 1850
5. July 26, 1858
6. Elizabeth Ruffin, 28, was enumerated by the U.S. Census in Norfolk on August 15, 1850, as the head of a household that included her three children William H. (6), Mary Jane (4), and Ottoway (2), as well as her sister, Mary Cornick, 32, and her grandmother, Hannah Cornick, who was 90. Mary Cornick was described as "mulatto", the others "black." None of the three adults could read or write. Mrs. Ruffin appears in the 1860 census with her three children, and in 1870 at 49, as a "domestic servant" with her husband Ottoway [Sr], a laborer, 56, as well as her sister Mary Cornick, 53, who is a seamstress. Also in the household were Mary Jane (24), a "washerwoman", her husband, William Keeling, 26, a "bar keeper", and their six month old son, William, Jr.; as well as Ottoway [Jr], 22, a barber, and his wife, Elizabeth, 19, who was a domestic servant. Elizabeth [the elder] and Mary could not read or write. Her husband Ottoway and the other adults could. All are described as "black" except for Ottoway's wife Elizabeth, Mary's husband William Keeling, and the baby, William Keeling, Jr., who are "mulatto." According to the records of West Point Cemetery in Norfolk, Elizabeth Ruffin died January 17, 1894, age 73, of "paralysis."

RUFFIN, MARY PATTERSON ("Mary Patterson, alias Mary Ruffin")

1. Born circa 1811

2. Height: 4'11½; "A negro woman of light black complexion with no apparent mark or scar on head, face or hands"
3. Born free in Norfolk
4. Norfolk, April 2, 1833 and October 30, 1838
5. September 27, 1852
6. According to the U.S. Federal Census Mortality Schedules of 1870, Mary Ruffin, age 58, female, black, died in Norfolk's Third Ward in June, 1869 of "consumption."

SALES, ELIZABETH
(Child of Susan Sales, formerly Wallace)

1. Born May, 1837
2. Height not taken [she was 10 months old]; Height: 4'8½" [1851, age 13]; "negro child of light complexion with mark on left shoulder" [1838]; "free negro girl of light black complexion" with "two marks or scars on the right hand, one near the first joint of the thumb and the other near the wrist" [1851]
3. Born free in Norfolk, proved by oath of R.B. Langley [1851]
4. Norfolk, March 27, 1838 and November 3, 1851
5. October 2, 1851 and July 26, 1858
6. "I am unable to state whether or not she is a descendant of a female slave emancipated since first day of May 1806" (Clerk, 1858).
An "Eliza" Sales, "mulatto", age 13, appears in the 1850 census in Norfolk, enumerated in the household of 25 year old mulatto Clara Hall.

SALES, GEORGE (George Wallace, alias Sales)
(Child of Susan Sales, formerly Wallace)

1. Born circa 1832
2. Height: 5'5¼"; "Negro boy of light black complexion" with "scar on nose near right corner of left eye, one near left corner of mouth, one on middle joint of right middle finger"
3. Born free in Norfolk, proved by oath of R.B. Langley
4. Norfolk, November 3, 1851
5. January 31, 1861

SALES, MITCHELL
(Child of Susan Sales, formerly Susan Wallace)

1. Born circa 1836
2. Height not taken [he was two]; "Negro child of light black complexion"
3. Born free in Norfolk
4. Norfolk, March 27, 1838
5. October 2, 1851

_____, **SALLY** [Surname not given]

1. Born circa 1801
2. Height: 5' ; "Negro woman of light black complexion"; missing "upper front teeth"
3. Emancipated in city of Norfolk by will of Ursula Sautigan, November 22, 1837
4. Norfolk, December 14, 1846
5. July 25, 1853

_____, **SALLY** [Surname not given]

1. Born circa 1808
2. Height: 5'3"; "Negro woman of black complexion" with "no visible marks or scars"
3. Emancipated in Norfolk by D.M. Curtis
4. Norfolk, February 20, 1850
5. January 28, 1861

_____, **SALLY** [Surname not given]

1. Born circa 1827
2. Height: 4'11½"; "Negro woman of black complexion" with "no apparent mark or scar"
3. Emancipated in city of Norfolk by will of Ann Taylor, June 26, 1854
4. Norfolk, August 29, 1854
5. January 31, 1861

_____, **SAM** [Surname not given]

1. Born circa 1809
2. Height: 5'10¼"; "Free negro man of black complexion" with "wart or mole near first joint of left little finger"

3. Emancipated by will of Ann Taylor, deceased, June 25, 1854
4. Norfolk, June 26, 1854 and January 29, 1855
5. January 23, 1860

SAMPLE, BETSEY

1. Born circa 1817
2. Height 5'3", "Dark complexion, scar on left cheek from cut"
3. Born free
4. Norfolk County, June 19, 1843
5. January 22, 1844

SAMPLE, CHARLOTTE

1. Born circa 1820
2. [In April, 1845] Height 5'6", "Woman of dark complexion, with scar near the right eye, from a cut, and one on the first joint of the thumb of the left hand, from a cut"; [in October, 1845]: Height" 5'5"; "black complexion" with "scar near right eye from cut and one on first joint o the thumb of left hand, from a cut."
3. Born free
4. Norfolk County, April 25, 1845; Norfolk October 30, 1845
5. October 30, 1845 and July 26, 1853

SAMPSON, MARTHA

1. Born circa 1824
2. Height: 5'3"; "Negro woman of dark complexion...[has] lost some of her lower front teeth."
3. Born free in Isle of Wight County, "removed therefrom to this city to labor herein"
4. Isle of Wight County, March 3, 1845; Norfolk, January 4, 1850
5. December 24, 1849 and July 26, 1858
6. According to the U.S. Census of 1870, a 45 year old Virginia-born Martha Sampson, black, was living in the Second Ward of Hamilton, Butler County, Ohio, with her husband, William, age 51, a teamster, and a three year old girl Laura, evidently a daughter or grand-daughter.

_____SARAH

The "register" has disintegrated to the point of illegibility.

3. Born free in Norfolk
5. July 26, 1858

SATCHELL, ATHA, see SATCHELL, LOUISA

SATCHELL, LOUISA

1. Born circa 1831
2. Height: 5'1½"; "Negro girl of black complexion" with "scar on the right arm above the rist [sic]" and "slightly pitted in the face with the smallpox" and "a small scar on the right hand"
3. Born free in Norfolk, proved by oath of James Cherry
4. Norfolk, July 25, 1850
5. July 26, 1858
[Miss Satchell is] "a child of Atha Satchell, an emancipated slave who appears from her register to have been emancipated in the County Court of Northampton by the will of Charles S. Satchell, December 9, 1805" (Clerk)

SATCHELL, PETER

1. Born circa 1820
2. Height 5'6 and seven tenths" ; "black complexion", "scar in middle of forehead, lips thick, two of upper front teeth out and some of others defective [he was 35], mole on the forefinger of the right hand"
3. Born free in Northampton County [VA]
4. Northampton County, June 20, 1855
5. July 31, 1858
6. The Census of 1850 shows Peter Satchell living in Eastville, Northampton County, on August 16. The household included:
    Mary Satchell, 35, female, black
    Peter Satchell, 23, male, black
    Betsey Satchell, 14, female, black
No occupation is listed for any of the three

SAUNDERS, ANN

1. Born circa 1809
2. Height: 5'3½"; "A negro woman of light complexion"

3. Emancipated in Norfolk by William Sharp, by deed.
4. Norfolk, July 22, 1833 and November 1, 1837
5. 1851
6. She had two children: Sylvia, born circa 1830 and Mary, born circa 1832, who are described as children "of mulatto complexion."

SAUNDERS, HARRIET

1. Born circa 1813
2. Height: 5'1½"; "Woman of mulatto complexion...mole near left ear and dark spot on ball of left eye" [1837]; "negro woman of light complexion" with "mole near left eye and dark spot on ball of left eye" [1850]
3. "Emancipated in Norfolk by William Sharp by deed bearing date of July 12, 1831, recorded August 21, 1835
4. Norfolk, November 1, 1837 and October 27, 1850
5. October 28, 1850 and July 26, 1858
6. "To whom permission has not been granted to remain in the Commonwealth by the said Court, or any other that I can ascertain." (Clerk, 1858)

SAUTIGAN, EDWARD
(Son of Sally, "a negro woman emancipated by Ursula Sautigan")

1. Born circa 1840
2. Height: 5'2½" [he was 13]; "black complexion"
3. Born free in Norfolk
4. Norfolk, July 25, 1853
5. July 26, 1858
6. "He is the descendant of a female slave emancipated since the 1 day of May 1806" (Clerk)

SAUTIGAN, SALLY

1. Age not given
2. Height: 5'¼"; "woman of black complexion" with "no apparent mark or scar on head, face, or hands" but with "upper front teeth" missing.
3. Emancipated in Norfolk by will of Ursula Sautigan, November 22, 1837
4. Norfolk, August 8, 1853

5. July 26, 1858

SCOTT, CHARLOTTE

1. Born circa 1788
2. Height: 5'2"; "Free woman of light complexion" with "scar near left ear"
3. Born free in Southampton County
4. Southampton County, July 21, 1834
5. No date

SCOTT, COUPLAND, see COUPLAND, SCOTT

SCOTT, JOSEPH

1. Born circa 1821
2. Height 5'7"; "Free man of mulatto complexion with no apparent scar on head, face, or hands"
3. Born free in Norfolk
4. Norfolk City, October 30, 1846
5. March 24, 1852

SCOTT, JOSEPH (JOE)
(Son of Milly Scott)

1. Born circa 1834
2. "Height is not taken in consequence of his youth", "Mulatto boy [with] no visible marks or scars on face or hands"
3. Evidently born free
4. Norfolk Borough, July 10, 1844
5. October 30, 1846

SCOTT, MARGARET ANN

1. Born circa 1829
2. Height: 4'11¾"; "A free girl of mulatto complexion" with "small black mole behind right ear"
3. Born free, proved by oath of Eliza Taylor
4. Norfolk, September 5, 1845
5. July 26, 1853

SCOTT, MINERVA

1. Born circa 1811
2. Height: 4'8" [1851]; 5'½ [1853]; "Negro woman of dark complexion" with "scar in the middle of her forehead"
3. "Born of a free negro woman" in Isle of Wight County, "having removed to this city."
4. Isle of Wight County, June 2, 1851; Norfolk, August 2, 1853
5. July 30, 1853 and February 2, 1861

SCOTT, MOSES
(Son of Milly Scott)

1. Born circa 1843
2. Height not taken, "Boy of black complexion, no visible scars"
3. Evidently born free
4. Norfolk, July 10, 1844
5. October 30, 1846

SEAMAN, ROBERT
(Son of Hannah)

1. Born circa 1832
2. Height: 5'7"; "Negro boy of light mulatto complexion" with "scar on left cheekbone and another on right arm, just above wrist"
3. Born free in Norfolk, proved by oath of Nancy West
4. Norfolk, April 3, 1850
5. October 31, 1856

SHANKS, WILLIAM

1. Born circa 1830
2. Height: 5'9"; "Negro man of black complexion" with "no apparent mark or scar on head, face, or hands"
3. Born free in Elizabeth City County
4. Norfolk, December 1, 1851
5. November 25, 1856
6. "From the best information that I can obtain [he is] a descendant of a female Negro who was born free."

SIMON, WESLEY

1. Born circa 1825
2. Height: 5'8½"; "Bright mulatto man, straight hair, first joint on finger next to little finger on right hand crooked, caused by sprain and forefinger is also crooked at first joint on same hand"
3. Born free
4. Norfolk, December 3, 1858
5. April 27, 1859

SINGLETON, ANN
(Daughter of Betsey Singleton)

1. Born circa 1820
2. Height: 5'2"; "Mulatto complexion"; "small mole on the right side of the neck, below the ear" [1845]; "Free woman of yellow complexion" with "small mole on right side of neck, below ear" [1853]
3. Born free in Norfolk, proved by oath of Elizabeth C. Donaldson
4. Norfolk, September 29, 1845 and August 8, 1853
5. July 26, 1853 and July 23, 1860

SMITH, ANN

1. Born circa 1825
2. Height: 5'3"; "Negro woman of black complexion" with "scar on her left wrist, near hand"
3. Born free in Norfolk County, proven by oath of Charles Manning
4. Norfolk, May 3, 1850
5. July 26, 1858
6. In her freedom register is an official "Discharge", which reads, "This is to certify that 139, Henry Smith, a hand, has this day been discharged from the U.S. Ship *Plymouth* and from the naval service, 23 January 1853, John Niceley , Captain

The U.S. Census of 1850 for the city of Norfolk shows that Ann Smith, age 27, black, was living with Allen Smith, 28, black, a laborer, who was evidently her husband, and three children, Joy (a 7 year old boy), Josephine (6), and Oliver (3), as well as two men who were apparently her unmarried brothers, Edward, 22, black and Henry (the seaman), 25, black.

SMITH, ARSENA (FORMERLY CUFFEE)

1. Born circa 1821
2. Height: 4'11"; "Negro woman of light mulatto complexion" with "scar just below left eye, from scratch"
3. Born free in Norfolk County, "removed therefrom to this City to labor therein"
4. Norfolk, April 3, 1850
5. August 3, 1858

SMITH, CHARLES

1. Born circa 1801
2. Height: 5'9¾, "A black man...with a scar on the left forefinger"
3. Born free in Princess Anne County
4. Princess Anne County, September 5, 1831
5. January 24, 1842

SMITH, HENRY

1. Born circa 1825
2. Height: 5'6"; "Man of black complexion"
3. Born free in Princess Anne County
4. [Illegible]
5. July 20, 1858
6. Enclosed in his "register" is the following document: "City of Norfolk, to wit: Henry Smith, a free negro man has this day exhibited his papers in a mutilated condition from having been injured by rain while he was at sea in the service of the United States 7 I find them to be dated 29th day of June 1855. See: Smith, Ann

SMITH, HENRY

1. Born circa 1826
2. Height: 5'9½"; "Bright mulatto man [with] small scar over left eye, from a cut."
3. Born free
4. Norfolk County, March 15, 1847
5. August 28, 1848

SMITH, JAMES

1. Born circa 1805
2. Height: 5'10"; "Free negro man of yellowish complexion" with "scar on left wrist, occasioned by a saw, and one on back of right hand, near joint of the wrist, occasioned by the bite of a dog."
3. Born free in Princess Anne County [VA]; "removed to this city to labor"
4. Princess Anne County, October 6, 1828; Norfolk, March 31, 1846 and August 21, 1853
5. November 29, 1845, July, 1853 and August 31, 1858

SMITH, JAMES

1. Born circa 1825
2. Height: 5'8¾"; "Dark complected negro man with his left eye out, with a scar on the right cheek, below the eye."
3. Born free in Princess Anne County
4. Princess Anne County, May 7, 1849
5. May 28, 1849

6. A James Smith appears in the U.S. Census of 1850, in Portsmouth Parish (November 1), in the household of John and Cecelia Perry, white. He is listed as a "labourer", 25, "black", and illiterate.

SMITH, JAMES

1. Born circa 1830
2. Height" 4'10"; "Boy of dark complexion, no marks or scars about his face or hands perceivable."
3. Born free "as appears from evidence of John J. Howell."
4. Henrico County, December 3, 1844
5. September 25, 1848
6. A James Smith, Jr., age 21, appears in the U.S. Census of St. Bride's Parish, Norfolk County, on September 10, 1850. He is the eldest of eight children of James Smith, Sr., a 50 year old "farmer."

SMITH, JOHN

1. Born circa 1822

2. 5'7½", "Negro man of dark complexion, with scar in the center of his forehead, over the nose"
3. Born free
4. Norfolk County, October 21, 1844
5. November 1, 1845

SMITH, LUCY

1. Born circa 1814
2. Height: 5'; "Negro woman of black complexion" with "pits or marks in the face, occasioned by smallpox"
3. Born free in Norfolk County, proved by oath of Mary Sessoms
4. Norfolk, January 30, 1850
5. July 26, 1858
6. A Lucy Smith, age 30, "mulatto", was enumerated by the U.S. Census in Norfolk City on August 5, 1850. She was the only person listed in her household; she could neither read nor write; no occupation is listed.

SMITH, NANCY

1. Born circa 1820
2. Height: 5'3"; "Woman of light complexion, small mole at bottom of right ear."
3. Born free
4. Norfolk County, October 22, 1839
5. October 28, 1848

SMITH, SARAH

1. Born circa 1824
2. Height: 5'5"; "Free mulatto woman" with "black mole on right side of neck"
3. Born free, proved by oath of John Forde, Jr.
4. Norfolk, August 6, 1847
5. July 26, 1853

SMITH, WILLIS

1. Born circa 1822
2. Height: 5'5 and five eights"; "Free negro man of black complexion"

with "scar on outer corner of left eyebrow"
3. Born free in Norfolk, proven by oath of George Bramble
4. Norfolk, August 6, 1853
5. July 26, 1858
6. "I am unable to state whether or not he is a descendant of a female slave emancipated since the first day of May, 1806" (Clerk)

SPARROW, AMY
(Daughter of Ellen Legrass)

1. Born 1842
2. Height not taken [she was eight]; "black complexion, small scar on each side of upper lip"
3. Born free in Norfolk, proved by oath of Joseph F. Allyn
4. Norfolk, January 28, 1850
5. July 26, 1858

SPARROW, JAMES

1. Born circa 1810
2. Height: 5'5½"; "Man of dark complexion" with "scar on left wrist from a burn and scar on the corner of his left eye"
3. Born free in Norfolk County
4. Norfolk County, September 19, 1831
5. March 29, 1838

SPARROW, JANE, see TOTTEN, JANE

SPARROW, JESSE

1. Born circa 1820-1821
2. Height 5'5¼" [in September, 1842], 5'5" [in November, 1842 and August, 1853] , "A black man with two scars on the left hand and wrist" [in September, 1842]; "A free negro man of black complexion" with "scar on the left hand between the first joints of the thumb and forefinger" and "small scar on left wrist."
3. Born free in Princess Anne County
4. Princess Anne County, September 5, 1842; Norfolk, November 3, 1842
5. October 25, 1842, July 25, 1853, and August 30, 1853
6. He appears in the 1850 census in the City of Norfolk, along with

family in Princess Anne County. Mary was described as 40 years old, and "black". The head of the household was Adam Sparrow, age 60, "black," who worked as a "labourer." He may have been either Mary's husband or father. Both Adam and Mary could read and write. There are four younger males listed—evidently Mary's children: William, 15; Robert, 13; Eddy, 9; and Stephen, 6. Mary had four sons:

SPARROW, NANCY

1. Circa 1821
2. Height 5'¾", "Bright mulatto woman with scar on upper lip and one on right hand" [1847]; "woman of light complexion" with "scar on upper lip and one on right hand"
3. Born free in Norfolk County
4. Norfolk County, June 19, 1843; Norfolk City, November 22, 1847 and July 25, 1853
5. November 22, 1847; again July 25, 1853 and August 23, 1858
6. "I hereby certify that I am well acquainted with Nancy Sparrow, the bearer thereof. She has been living in the city of Norfolk for three or four years and during that time has remained upon my lot. She is a woman of orderly and good habits." (Virginia A. Newcomb, November 22, 1847)
"I am well acquainted with the above named Nancy Sparrow and she is the same woman found in the accompanying register from the clerk of Norfolk County, dated 26 February 1845." (Horatio N. Burkhart)

"I am unable to state whether or not she is a descendant of a female slave emancipated since first day of May 1806" (Clerk, 1853)

SPARROW, NED

1. Born circa 1808
2. Height: 5'3¼"; "Black man" with "scar on left arm from cut"
3. Born free
4. Norfolk County, September 30, 1831
5. November 29, 1837
6. Ned Sparrow may have moved to New York. On October 28, 1850, the U.S. Census recorded an Edward Sparrow, 43, black, and Virginia-born, working as a laborer in the Fourth Ward of New York

(Manhattan). He had a wife, Charity, age 33, black, born in North Carolina, and, living with them as a 14 year old boy, John Henry, perhaps Charity's son, born in Virginia.

SPARROW, SARAH FRANCES
(Daughter of Jane Totten)

1. Born circa 1847
2. "Girl of black complexion" with "scar on right side of forehead and another near corner of right eye"
3. Born free in Norfolk, proved by oath of Elizabeth Donaldson
4. Norfolk, March 5, 1850
5. July 26, 1858

SPARROW, TOM

1. Born circa 1826
2. Height: 5'6½; "Negro man of dark complexion with a scar on the chin"
3. Born free in Princess Anne County
4. Norfolk City, January 24, 1848 and September 7, 1853
5. July 25, 1853 and August 31, 1858
6. Accompanying Sparrow's freedom papers is a note which reads, "Sarah Dempsey has permission to remain here till the steamer *Herbert* comes back and if anybody bothers her, she is authorised to call on Mr. Sparrow as she is the wife of my fireman come out to see her husband.
October 16, 57, E[lizabeth] City, H.B. Hopkins

SPRATLEY, CHRISTIANA

1. Born circa 1836
2. Height: 5'1"; "Free negro," "light complexion, scar on her right arm"
3. Born free in Surry County, certified by "Benjamin N. Epps, a white man"
4. Surry County, May 28, 1856
5. July 26, 1858

SPRATLEY, LUCINDA

1. Born circa 1828
2. Height: 5'2 and five eights"; "Negro woman of brown complexion, thin visage" with "no apparent marks or scars on face, head, or hands"
3. Born free in Surry County and "removed therefrom to this city to labor therein"
4. Norfolk, May 31, 1850
5. July 27, 1858

STEPHENS, AMY

1. Born December, 1816
2. Height: 5'1 and one fifth"; "Black complexion" with "short broad face, scar about half an inch long over left eyebrow, a small mole in the palm of each hand.
3. Born free in Northampton County
4. Northampton County, May 10, 1854
5. July 31, 1858

Amy Stephens, according to the U.S. Census of August 15, 1850, was living in Northumberland County. The household included Amy, the head, who was 40 years old and "black", as well as:

> Patience Stephens, 28, female, black
> Frisby Stephens, 8, male, black
> Catharine Stephens, 9 female, black
> Patrick Collins, 30, male, black
> Richard Stephens, 7, male, black
> George Stephens, 5, male black
> John Stephens, 11 months, male, black
> William Stephens, 24, male, black.

The only adult for whom an occupation is stated is William Stephens, who was a laborer. None of the family could read or write.

STEPHENS, HARRY

1. Born June 13, 1814
2. Height: 5'5 and three tenths"; "Complexion yellow" with "soft woolly hair, freckled about the nose and eyes, sundry moles or perhaps freckles on back of neck, two moles on right side of under lip, full face, stout and strong-made"
3. Born free in Northampton County
4. Northampton County, May 8, 1837
5. May 3, 1838

STEPHENS, ROSEY

1. Born December 25, 1831
2. Height: 5'1 and three tenths"; "Bright mulatto" with "long mark resembling a scratch on left cheek, beginning near outer corner of left and extending about two inches towards the jaw, wide mouth, thick lips, broad nose"
3. Born free in Northampton County [VA]
4. Northampton, April 9, 1849
5. July 31, 1858

STEPHENS, SALLY

1. Born May 4, 1824
2. Height: 5'¾"; "Free negro woman of black complexion, having a scar on the inside of the bottom joint of the thumb of her left hand, a small mole on the neck under the right jaw, a round scar on each knee about 7/16th of a inch in diameter, a small scar on the upper part of the left breast and a short, flat nose.
3. Born free in Northampton County
4. Norfolk City, September 26, 1845
5. September 27, 1852

STEPHENS, WILLIAM

1. "Born about July, 1829"
2. Height: 5'4 and 6/10ths"; "Mulatto...scar on top of nose, cut across in the shape of a half circle, about the size of a dime, small round scar on back part of neck just below the hair and a mole about an inch to the left of this scar."
3. Not stated
4. Northampton County, October 9, 1848
5. March 26, 1849

STEVENS, ROBERT SPEED

1. Born January 5, 1817
2. Height: 5'10"; "Dark brown complexion, small scar on his nose nearly in a parallel line with his eyes and another somewhat larger on the back of his left hand"

3. Born free
4. Petersburg, September 6, 1834
5. May 16, 1835
6. "By trade a blacksmith"
The U.S. Census of 1870 shows a Virginia-born Robert Stevens, age 50, living in the Third Ward of Boston, Massachusetts, working as a "wood and coal dealer". He had a wife Sarah, 38, also Virginia-born, who kept house, and three children, William (15), Augusta (6), and George, (five months), all born in Massachusetts. The Stevenses were "mulatto" and neither parent could read or write. The oldest son was "at school."

STOKELEY, LEAH

1. Born 1804
2. Height: 5'1½" [1830]; 5'2¼" [1851]; "a black rather inclining to yellow, small scar on the inside of right arm, occasioned by a burn" [1830]; "free negro woman" with "small scar on inside part of right arm, near joint of elbow" [1852]
3. "Born free in Accomack County [VA] in 1804 and removed to this city to labor therein" [1852]
4. Accomack County, July 26, 1830; Norfolk, September 30, 1840 and September 30, 1851
5. November 24, 1851 and July 26, 1858

STUBBS, AMELIA, see STUBBS, MILLY

STUBBS, GEORGIANA
(Daughter of Milly Stubbs)

1. Born circa 1832
2. Height: 5'; "Free negro girl of black complexion" with "scar on left side of face and scar in left eyebrow"
3. Born free in Norfolk, proven by oath of Eliza Dowdy
4. Norfolk, February 18, 1850
5. July 26, 1858
See Stubbs, Milly

STUBBS, MARGARET
(Daughter of Milly Stubbs)

1. Born circa 1833
2. Height: 5'½"; "Free negro girl of black complexion" with "no apparent marks or scars"
3. [?]
4. Norfolk, February 18, 1850
5. July 26, 1858
6. "She is allowed to go at large until next Court, Wm W. Lamb, Mayor, July 21, 1858"
See Stubbs, Milly

STUBBS, MARY ANN
(Daughter of Milly Stubbs, free negro woman)

1. Born circa 1830
2. Height: 5'2½"; "free negro girl" with "several small scars about the wrist of right arm, black mole on neck"
3. Born free in Norfolk, proved by oath of Eliza Dowdy
4. Norfolk, July 30, 1840 and February 18, 1850
5. August 26, 1856
6. See Stubbs, Milly

STUBBS, MILLY (actually AMELIA)

1. Born circa 1813
2. Height: 5'8¾"; "free negro woman of light black complexion" with "scar on forehead near the hair and a black mole in the corner of left eye"
3. Born free in Norfolk, proven by oath of Eliza Dowdy
4. Norfolk, July 30, 1840 and February 18, 1850
5. July 26, 1858
The household was enumerated in the 1850 census of the city of Norfolk. Headed by the mother Amelia "Milly", age 47, black, it included Mary A. Brown, age 21, evidently a married daughter, with Mary's daughter, 4 year old Sarah A. Brown. Also living in the household were Milly's daughters Georgianna, 18, and Margaret F, 17. Amelia and Mary could not read or write, but Georgianna and Margaret could. No occupation is listed for any members of the family. Georgiana [her name is sometimes spelled with two "n"s and sometimes one) appears with her mother in the 1870 census. They

were living in Norfolk City in the household of William Carter, a 40 year old laborer, and his wife, Lucy A., who was 35. The Carters had three children: Lewis, 16, Emily 4, and Lucy A., 2. Georgiana, then 38, was married to William Tyler, a 35 year old laborer. Besides Amelia, whose age is given as 53, the household includes a one year old child, Mary Jackson. All are described as "black." William Carter could not read or write, but the others could.

SULLEATHER, JANE

1. Born circa 1827
2. Height: 4'½" [she was 10]; "High mulatto" with "no mark or scar perceptible"
3. Born free, on evidence of James Roy Micon, Jr.
4. Essex County, June 19, 1837
5. February 26, 1838

SULLEATHER, PATSEY

1. Born circa 1791
2. Height: 5'1 and one eighth; "Dark mulatto color" with "tolerable bushy hair and somewhat grey"
3. Born free

4. Essex County, June 19, 1837
5. February 28, 1838

_____, SUSAN [Surname not given]

1. Born circa 1840
2. Height: 4'9¼"; "Free girl of light black complexion" with "no mark or scar on head, face, or hands"
3. Emancipated by the will of Ann Taylor, deceased, admitted to probate June 26, 1854
4. Norfolk, August 7, 1854
5. December 3, 1859

TAYLOR, CHARLES FRANCIS
(son of Clementine Lumlet)

1. Born circa 1836

2. "Height not taken" because of age; "Bright mulatto complexion, no apparent mark or scar on head, face, or hands, small mole on back of neck."
3. Emancipated by deed by William Taylor, April 26, 1841
4. Norfolk, August 11, 1842
5. July, 1853
6. Charles Taylor evidently died between 1842 and June, 1850, when his mother and siblings were enumerated in the U.S. Census

[TAYLOR], CLEMENTINE, see LUMLET, CLEMENTINE

TAYLOR, EDMUND

1. Born circa 1812
2. Height: 5'8¾; "No apparent mark or scar on head, face, or hands"
3. Emancipated by will of William Deans in 1801
4. Norfolk County, January 10, 1832; Norfolk Borough June 20, 1833
5. July 26, 1853

TAYLOR, EDWARD
("Son of Emily Taylor, free mulatto woman")

1. Born circa 1837
2. "Height not taken in consequence of his youth"; "Negro boy of light black complexion"

3. Born free in Norfolk Borough, proven by oath of Charles H. Smith and Ann Grey
4. Norfolk City, March 24, 1846
5. May 26, 1851

TAYLOR, EMILY, see WHITE, WILLIAM

TAYLOR, JUSTINE
("Daughter of Emily Taylor, free woman of color")

1. Born circa 1843
2. Height not taken [She was three]. "A girl three years of age, light black complexion"
3. Born free in Norfolk, proven by oath of Charles H. Smith and Ann Grey

4. Norfolk, March 24, 1846

5. May 26, 1851

TAYLOR, MARY LOUISA
(daughter of Clementine Lumlet)

1. Born circa 1839 or 1840

2. "Height not taken" because of age [1842]; Height:4'11¾ [1853]; "Bright mulatto complexion, straight hair, two small moles, one on right and two on left side of face [1842]"; "Girl of bright mulatto complexion" with "small mole in the middle of forehead, another small mole on the right cheek, and another small mole on left side of face, near the nose"

3. Emancipated by deed by William Taylor, April 26, 1841

4. Norfolk, August 11, 1842 and August 23, 1853

5. July, 1853 and July 26, 1858

6. She appears in the U.S. Census of 1860, living with her mother, Clementine Taylor in the city of Norfolk. Also in the household were her sisters Clementine (16) and Zeli (13), and 3 year old Mary Stokes, who appears to have been a niece. All family members were described as "mulatto."

TAYLOR, SARAH ANN
(Daughter of Clementine Lumlet)

1. Born circa 1834 or 1835

2. "Height not taken" on account of age" [1841]; 5'1 and three eighths" [1853] "Very bright mulatto complexion with straight hair, small mole in the right eyebrow" [1841]; "Bright mulatto complexion, small mole on right cheek and another on left side of face near the nose" [1853]

3. Emancipated by deed by William Taylor, April 26, 1841

4. Norfolk, August 23, 1853

5. July, 1853 and July 26, 1858

See Lumlet, Clementine

TAYLOR, WILLIAM
("Son of Emily Taylor, free mulatto woman")

1. Born circa 1839

2. "Height not taken" [he was 7]; " A boy...of mulatto complexion,

having straight black hair, a scar near the outer corner of his left eye, and three small scars on the back of right hand"
3. Born free in Norfolk, proved by oath of Charles H. Smith and Ann Grey
4. Norfolk, March 24, 1846
5. May 26, 1851

TEMER, NANCY

1. Born circa 1785
2. Height: 5'¾"; "Negro woman of black complexion with small scar on back of left hand, marked in the face with the smallpox"
3. Born free in Nansemond County [VA}
4. Norfolk, August 27, 1835
5. June 23, 1851

TEMERS, JESSE

1. Born circa 1809
2. Height: 5'6½"; "Man of light complexion" with "small scar on left arm, a little above the wrist, and one on the breast"
3. Born of free parents in Isle of Wight County

4. Isle of Wight County, August 11, 1834
5. September 22, 1834

THOMPSON, GEORGE

1. "Born June 3, 1824"
2. Height: 5'8½"[1844]; 5'9½" [1848]; "Dark color, scar on left side of left eyebrow; scar on right arm near shoulder; small mole on right side of neck; large scar on right leg on joint above ankle bone on the outside; scar on left knee; carries head well up—likely" [1844]; "Negro man of black complexion" with "scar on the left eyebrow, another scar on right arm near the should, a small mole on the right side of the neck, large scar on right leg, just above the ankle bone on the outside and another scar on left knee" [1848]
3. Born free in Northampton County [VA], "removed therefrom to this city to labor therein"
4. Northampton County, October 14, 1844; Norfolk, July 18, 1848
5. January 24, 1848 and April 27, 1854

6. George Thompson, a laborer, age 25, black, illiterate, appears in the U.S. Census of the "City of Norfolk" September 30, 1850, living alone.

THOROGOOD, CHARLOTTE

1. Born circa 1814
2. Height: 5'2½'; "Negro woman of black complexion" with "large scar on the outer side of left arm, between elbow and wrist."
3. Born free in Norfolk
4. Norfolk, September 8, 1835
5. November 24, 1851
6. She had two children: James Henry Thorogood, age 2 [born circa 1833], described as of "light black complexion with reddish mark behind right ear"; and Mary Eliza Thorogood, two months old [born June or July 1835], of "light black complexion"

THOROUGHGOOD, NANCY

1. Born circa 1829
2. Height: 5'½"; "Negro woman of black complexion" with "scar on the back of right hand"
3. Born free in Norfolk, proved by oath of Elizabeth Connor

4. Norfolk, April 20, 1850
5. July 26, 1858

THOROUGHGOOD, PEGGY

1. Born circa 1808
2. Height: 5'1½"; "Woman of dark mulatto complexion" with "a cut in her forehead just above left eye, occasioned by a scratch or cut; right and left little fingers are crooked so that they cannot be perfectly straightened"
3. Born free in Princess Anne County
4. Norfolk, June 26, 1838
5. July 25, 1853
6. Peggy Thorogood appears in the U.S. Census for the city of Norfolk, July 31, 1860. Her age is given as 42 (ten years younger than that given on her register) and her color as black. Living with her is 20 year old Nancy Thorogood, a "mulatto", evidently a daughter. No occupations are given for either of them.

THOROUGHGOOD, SALLY

1. Born circa 1819
2. Height: 5'1 and seven eighths"; "Negro woman of black complexion" with "small scar on forehead and another on left side of forehead near the hair and one on the left wrist."
3. Born free in Norfolk County
4. Norfolk, August 15, 1853
5. January 28, 1861
6. "I am unable to ascertain whether or not she is the descendant of a female negro emancipated after first day of May 1806" (Clerk, 1853)
   "Application for renewal to be made at next court, Wm. W. Lamb, Mayor, January 15, 1861"
   According to the U.S. Census, on August 8, 1860, Sally "Thorogood" was living in the City of Norfolk. Her age is given as 42, her color as "black", her occupation as "laundress." She had a personal estate of $60. Living with her are three younger people who appear to be her children:
   Joseph, age 20, "black", who was working as a "boatman," and two daughters with no listed occupation, Eliza and Margaret, age 19 and 12, both described as "black."

THOROWGOOD, BETSEY
(Daughter of Patty Thorowgood)

1. Born circa 1820
2. Height: 5'4"[1838], 5½" [1953]; "Negro woman of black complexion" with :scar under the right jaw, occasioned by a burn" [1838]; "Free negro woman of black complexion" with "scar on right side of neck, under jaw and one on right collar bone" [1853]
3. Born free in Princess Anne County , proved by oath of Bagwell Moore
4. Norfolk, July 23, 1838 and August 15, 1853
5. July 26, 1853 and January 28, 1861
6. "I am unable to ascertain whether or not she is the descendant of a female negro emancipated since first day of May 1806" (Clerk, 1853)
   On August 8, 1860, Betsy "Thorogood" , age 36, "black",was, according to the U.S. Census, living in the city of Norfolk. With her were Lewis Tucker, 30, "mulatto", a laborer with a personal estate valued at $350, and Richard, Sarah, Hannah, and Samuel Thorogood,

ages 10, 7, 4, and 1, respectively, all "black."

THOROWGOOD, CHARLOTTE

1. Born circa 1815
2. Height not given. "Black woman...with a large scar on her left arm"
6. "Daughter of Tamar, a slave who belonged to John Thorowgood, who by his will dated 28th of July 1786 leaves her free after the death of his sister Anne Phipps, who I also certify to have died more than thirty years since and consequently Charlotte, the bearer of this paper was born at least two years after the requirement of Thorowgood's will setting her mother Young Tamar free took place.
21 August 1835

Ann Forde

THOROWGOOD, JOSEPH
(Son of Sally Thorowgood)

1. Born February 6, 1838
2. Height: 5'¼ [at 15]; "Free negro boy of black complexion" with "no apparent mark or scar"
3. Born free in Norfolk, proved by oath of Edward Decornis
4. Norfolk, August 15, 1853
5. January 28, 1861
6. "Application for renewal to be made to next court Wm. W. Lamb, Mayor, January 18, 1861"

THOROWGOOD, MOSES
(Son of Savina)

1. Born circa 1800
2. Height: 5'6½"; "Black man of dark complexion" with "scar across nose"
3. Emancipated by will of John Thorowgood, record in Princess Anne County
4. Princess Anne County, September 5, 1836
5. August 29, 1837
6. *"I Horatio Moore do certify that I have been acquainted with Moses Thorowgood, a free man of colour, for the last twelve years. The said Moses was in my employ and is one of the best Negroes I*

know. Moses has been a resident of the Borough ever since I knew him, having a wife in town belonging to Langley's estate who was alive within twelve months and I have not heard that she is dead. Norfolk Aug. 29 '37"

TIMBERLAKE, JOHN

1. Born circa 1825
2. Height: 5'8"; "Bright mulatto man [with] mark on right cheek
3. Born free
4. Norfolk County, July 16, 1849
5. June 26, 1850
6. John Timberlake appears in the 1850 census for Norfolk, Virginia. He is described as a laborer, aged 25, a mulatto, illiterate and he is enumerated with what appear to have been his wife, Sarah, mulatto, age 26, and their son, Dymetrios, eight months, as well as Sarah Fentress, age 52, mulatto (perhaps his mother-in-law), and Lydia Moss, age 14, black.

TIMBERLAKE, JULIA ANN

1. Born circa 1828
2. Height: 5'1"; "Bright mulatto" with "scar on the upper lip and one under right eye, from cuts"
3. Born free in Norfolk County
4. Norfolk, December 24,1850
5. July 31,, 1858

TOM

("Son of Tamer, a free woman of color")

1. Born circa 1827
2. Height" 5'5"; 'Negro man of black complexion" with "scar on third joint of first finger of right hand and another scar on left hand between first finger and thumb"
3. Born free in Norfolk
4. Norfolk, July 9, 1849
5. August 26, 1856

TOTTEN, ANN ELIZABETH
[Register is disintegrated and partly illegible]

(Daughter of Esther Totten)

1. Age 22
2. Height: 5' and one eighth"; mulatto complexion, scar on nose
3. Born free in Norfolk
4. May [day and year illegible]
5. September 23, 1861

TOTTEN, ESTHER

1. Born circa 1817
2. Height: 4'10¾"; "A free negro woman of rather light complexion" with "scar near centre of the underlip and a considerable beard"
3. Born free in Norfolk, as proved by oath of Horatio Moore
4. Norfolk, August 23, 1842
5. 1853
6. Totten had a daughter, Elizabeth Totten, aged "about six" [born circa 1836], "of mulatto complexion" with "straight hair" and no marks

TOTTEN, JANE

1. Born circa 1831
2. Height: 5'½"; "Woman of black complexion" with "no apparent mark or scar"
3. Born free in Norfolk, proved by oath of Elizabeth Donaldson
4. Norfolk, March 5, 1850
5. July 26, 1858
6. She had a child, Sarah Frances Sparrow, born circa 1847
She appears in the 1850 census as Jane Sparrow, the wife of Jesse Sparrow. Jesse was 30 years old; Jane was 25; and Sarah was 4. All are listed as "black."

TROTTER, MARGARET of [Register for 1838 is crumbled and partially illegible]

1. Born circa 1812
2. Height: 5'3½"; "Woman of brown complexion, mole on each side of face" [1837]
3. Born free in Nansemond County [VA]
4. Nansemond County, October 9, 1837; Norfolk, April, 1838

5. January 24, 1838 and July 31, 1858

TROTTER, SARAH

1. Born circa 1828
2. Height: 5'2¾"; "Mulatto girl" with "scar on forehead, between eyes, and small cut on finger"
3. Born free in Norfolk, proven by oath of Martha Ann Dawley
4. Norfolk, July 3, 1851
5. July 31, 1858
6. "I am unable to state whether or not she is a descendant of a female slave emancipated since first day of May 1806"
Sarah Trotter appears in the U.S. Census of 1850 in Norfolk City. Her age is given as 19, her color as "mulatto." She was living with her five month old mulatto daughter, Sarah C. Trotter.

TURNER, ELIZABETH

1. Born circa 1797
2. Height: 5'1½"; "free woman of color of black complexion" with "mole on the nuckle [sic] of her right wrist"
3. Emancipated by deed from Simon Turner, recorded in Surry County [VA]
4. Surry County, May 23, 1836
5. September 28, 1837

TURNER, MARY D.

1. Born circa 1822
2. Height: 4'9" [at 14]; "Free girl of color" "pocked-marked"
3. Emancipated by deed from Simon Turner, recorded in Surry County [VA]
4. Surry County, May 23, 1836
5. September 28, 1837

TURNER, SIMON

1. Born circa 1819
2. Height 5'2" [at 17]; "Free boy of color"; "dark complection with scar over right eye"
3. Emancipated by deed from Simon Turner, recorded in Surry

County [VA]
4. Surry County, May 23, 1836
5. September 28, 1837

TYNES, BIBANNA

1. Born circa 1823
2. Height: 5'1"; "Negro woman of dark complexion [with] small scar on left cheek bone and small mole on chin"
3. Born free in Isle of Wight County
4. Isle of Wight County, April 13, 1844
5. March 30, 1850

TYNES, CATY, see COCKE, CATY

TYNES, CHARLES

1. Born circa 1802
2. Height: 5'7"; "Negro man of lightish complexion (for a negro)" with "scar on left arm a little above the bent or his arm, also another scar on the nose, near the end, round, full face"
3. Born free in Isle of Wight County
4. Isle of Wight County, July 18, 1830
5. No date

TYNES, CHARLES

1. Born circa 1822
2. Height: 5'3¾" [at 16]; "Boy of black complexion" with "scar on forehead," scar "just above the lips, rather large, and one or two on his forehead, scar on his left wrist, and prominent lips"
3. Born free in Isle of Wight County
4. Norfolk, July 11, 1838
5. July 26, 1858
6. "Allowed to go free till next Court, Wm. W. Lamb, Mayor, July 28, 1858"

TYNES, DIZE

1. Born circa 1813
2. Height: 5'5"; "Woman of bright complexion"

3. "Born of free parents", Isle of Wight County
4. Isle of Wight County, January 5, 1835
5. No date

TYNES, HARRIET

1. Born circa 1813
2. Height: 5'2"; "Free negro woman of bright complexion" with "scar on left jaw"
3. Born of free parents
4. Isle of Wight County, January 5, 1835
5. No date

TYNES, HARRY

1. Born c. 1791
2. Height: 5'8"; "negro man of dark complexion" with "no particular mark or scar"
3. Emancipated by the last will and testament of Timothy Tynes, Isle of Wight County, June 7, 1802
4. Isle of Wight County, January 16, 1835
5. No date

TYNES, HESTER
(Daugher of Patsy Godwin)

1. Born circa 1828
2. Height: 5'1"; "free negro girl of light black complexion," with "no apparent mark or scar on face, head, or hands" but has "lost two of her upper teeth" [1852]; "Free negro woman of light black complexion" with "small scar on right corner of right eye, mole on left cheek" and "has lost all upper front teeth" [1853]
3. Born free in Norfolk, as proved by oath of Eliza Thomas
4. Norfolk, November 1, 1852 and September 17, 1853
5. July 25, 1852 and December 26, 1860
6. "I am unable to ascertain whether she is a descendant of a free negro woman emancipated since the first day of May 1806" (Clerk, 1853)

TYNES, JENNY

1. Born circa 1809
2. Height: 5'1"; "Girl of dark complexion" with "scar on the back of left hand"
3. Emancipated by Charles Tynes, Isle of Wight County, February 7, 1825
4. Isle of Wight County, September 8, 1835
5. March 27, 1838
6. Ms. Tynes' freedom papers state that she had a daughter, Sarah, 9 years old in 1838

Enclosed in her papers is the deed by which she was freed:

Know all men by these presents that I Charles Tynes executor of Sam Tynes, dec'd, of the county of Isle of Wight and State of Virginia having under my care and management by virtue of the last will and Testament of the said Sam Tynes, dec'd the following named Negroes, to wit, Sarah, Eliza, Jenny, Merit & William Henry, son of said Eliza who were born and have been heretofore held as slaves and being fully persuaded that freedom is the natural right of all mankind and that it is my duty to do to others as I would desire to be done unto in the like situation do therefore emancipate and set free the said negroes Sarah, Eliza, Jenny, Merit& William Henry and their future increase and do for myself my heirs, executors and administrators relinquish all my right title, interest, and claim or pretention of claim, whatsoever either to their persons or to any estate they may hereafter acquire, the aforementioned nigroes [sic] and their future increase to enjoy their full freedom without any interruption from me or any persons claiming by from or under me. In Witness whereof I have hereunto set my hand & signed this 22d day of January 1825.

his
Charles X Tynes
mak

State of Virginia,
   Isle of Wight County (to wit)
   I Nathaniel Young clerk of the county aforesaid do hereby certify that at a court held for the said county of Isle of Wight the seventh day of February 1825 the foregoing deed of emancipation was acknowledged in court by Charles Tyes the party thereto and ordered to be recorded. In Testimony whereof I have hereunto set my hand

and affixed the seal of my office this 8ᵗʰ day of February 1825.

Nathl. Young

TYNES, JENNY

1. Born circa 1813
2. Height: 5'7"; "Negro woman of light complexion" with "no visible mark or scar"
3. "Born of free parents"
4. Isle of Wight County, January 21, 1835
5. No date

TYNES, JIM

1. Circa 1813-1814
2. Height 5'11½" [IN 1839]; 5'11¼" [in 1855] "A negro man of dark complexion...with a scar on his left eyelid near the eyebrow, occasioned by extracting a screw [?], one scar on the back of his left hand, and another scar on the same hand between the wrist and the first joint of his thumb" [1839]; "Free negro man of black complexion" with "scar on left eyelid near eye, occasioned by extraction of a wen, one on back of left hand and another on same hand between wrist and first joint of thumb and one on underlip, has lost one of the upper front teeth and who is marked on the face by smallpox" [1855]
3. Born free in Isle of Wight County [VA], "removed to this city"
4. Isle of Wight County, July 15, 1839; Norfolk, September 10, 1849 and October 19, 1855
5. May 24, 1841 and July 31, 1860
6. "Application to be made to Corp Court 4ᵗʰ Monday in August for renewal of Register, Wm. W. Lamb, Mayor, Norfolk, July 30, 1860" James Tynes appears in the U.S. Census of 1850 in the city of Norfolk, along with his wife and children:

    James Tynes, 40, male, black, measurer
    Eliza Tynes, 26, female, mulatto
    Louisianna Tynes, 8, female, black
    Rosetta Tynes, 3, female, black
    Mary Jane Tynes, 1, female, black
    James H. Tynes, 9, male, black
Neither parent could read or write.

TYNES, LIZZY

1. Born circa 1813
2. Height: 5'5"; "a Negro woman of light black complexion" with "no apparent marks or scars on her face, head, or hands."
3. Born [free?] in Isle of Wight County
4. Norfolk, December 2, 1837
5. July 26, 1853
6. According to the U.S. Census of 1850, Lizzy Tynes, "black", age 35, was living in the Eastern District of Isle of Wight County, along with Moses Tynes, "black", age 35, a farmer with property valued at $200, who was evidently her husband. The couple had four children: William H. (11), Louisa (12), Peter (9), and Rose (7).

TYNES, LOUISA

1. Born circa 1819
2. Height: 4'10¾"[at 16]; 4'11¼" [at 34]; "Negro girl of black complexion" with "small scar in right eye" [1835]; "Woman of black complexion" with "small scar in right eyebrow and another across the nose" [1853
3. Born free in Norfolk
4. Norfolk, August 31, 1835 and July 25, 1853
5. July 25, 1853 and August 24, 1853
6. "I am unable to state whether she is the descendant of a female Negro emancipated since the first day of May 1806"

TYNES, LOUISA
(Daughter of Patsy Tynes)

1. Born circa 1841
2. Height: 4'6¼" [at 11]; "Negro girl of black complexion" with "two small scars on right cheek and one on forehead"
3. Born free in Norfolk, proven by oath of Eliza Thomas
4. Norfolk, August 23, 1842
5. July 28, 1858

TYNES, LUCY ANN

1. Born circa 1820
2. Height: 5'1¾"; "Negro woman of dark complexion."

3. Born free in Isle of Wight County and "removed therefrom to this city to labour therein"

4. Isle of Wight County, March 2, 1847; Norfolk, July 6, 1849

5. July 9, 1849 and June 30, 1855

TYNES, MINERVA
(Daughter of Patsy Godwin)

1. Born circa 1821

2. Height: 5'4½"; "A free negro woman of black complexion" with "scar on left cheek, one in the middle joint of right little finger, and one on right wrist"; missing "one of her upper front teeth."

3. Born free in Norfolk, proved by oath of Eliza Thomas

4. Norfolk, November 1, 1842

5. July 25, 1853

6. Minerva Tynes was the wife of a slave, Joseph Camp. In the U.S. Census of 1860, on August 9, she appears in the city of Norfolk as the head of a large household. Her age is given (erroneously) as 3; her occupation as "seamstress". She was living with her 72 year old mother-in-law, Lydia Camp and seven children: William F. (13); Joseph [Jr.] (11); John (10); Bud [Timothy] (7); Alexander (6); Raymond (5), and Harriet, three months.

TYNES, MINERVA
(Daughter of Harriet Tynes the Elder)

1. Born circa 1829

2. Height: 4'11¾"; "Negro woman of black complexion" with "scar on right foot, near great toe"

3. Born free in County of Isle of Wight [VA], oath of Benjamin Cofer and Conney Brassey

4. Norfolk, September 7, 1850

5. July 26, 1858

TYNES, PATIENCE
(Register partially missing)

1. Born [according to census records] circa 1790

2. Height: 5'3" "Dark complexion" "very large and fat"

3. Freed by deed of Timothy Tynes

4. Isle of Wight County

5. Missing

6. The U.S. Census of 1850 reveals Patience Tynes, age 60, black, living with Matthew Artiste, 65, black, a fisherman, in the Eastern District of Isle of Wight County.

TYNES, PETER
(Son of Phillis Tynes)

1. Born circa 1817
2. Height: 5'7½"; "Negro boy of black complexion" with "mark on his right arm, near elbow"
3. Born free in Isle of Wight County, proved by oath of Conney Brassey (or Bassett?) and Benjamin Cofer
4. Norfolk, January 29, 1838 and July 26, 1853
5. July 26, 1853 and January 28, 1861
6. "I am unable to state whether he is a descendant of a female negro emancipated since the first day of May 1806" (Clerk, 1853)

Peter Tynes appears in the 1850 census in Norfolk. His age is given as "30", his color as "black", his trade as "oysterman." Living with him were Louise. She was aged 20 years and black. Also in the household was 34 year old Robert Tynes, "black", also an "oysterman." None of the three could read or write.

TYNES, PHILLIS

1. Born circa 1787
2. Height: 5'1"; "Negro woman of light complexion"
3. "Liberated by last will and testament of Timothy Tynes, deceased, June 7, 1802, Isle of Wight County"
4. Isle of Wight County, September 30, 1831
5. No date
6. Enclosed in Phillis Tynes' freedom papers is a copy of the will of Timothy Tynes, which reads, in part: *"In the name of God, Amen. I, Timothy Tynes do make and ordain this to be my last Will and Testament in the following manner, to wit, My Will and desire is that my Negroe named Phillis be fully and freely liberated from slavery and stand discharge from all Slavery and bondage, and her increase forever to enjoy all the privileges that free Negroes are entitled to by the laws and regulations of the State of Virginia." (May 9, 1802)"* Notation on Phillis Tynes' freedom papers:"She is dead—her [children?] are to be registered" (1837)

TYNES, ROBERT

1. Born circa 1816
2. Height: 5'10" [in 1837]; 5'11¼" [in 1853]; "Negro boy of dark complexion"; with "a small dent near the right ear, a great many small scars on the back part of both hands, occasioned by a burn."
3. Born free in Isle of Wight County, proved by Conney Brassey
4. Norfolk, June 27, 1837 and August 19, 1853
5. July 26, 1853 and January 28, 1861
6. In the U.S. Census of 1850, Robert Tynes, age 34, "black", an "oysterman" was living in Norfolk with Peter and Louisa Tynes, who appear to have been his brother and sister-in-law.

TYNES, SARAH, see TYNES, JENNY

TYNES, SUSAN

1. Born circa 1824
2. Height 5'3¼", "Negro woman of light complexion [with] long, bushy hair"
3. Born free in Isle of Wight County
4. Isle of Wight County, October 6, 1845; Norfolk, November 1, 1845
5. July 25, 1853

TYNES, TIMOTHY
(Son of Harriet Tynes the Younger)

1. Born circa 1830
2. Height not taken (he was 8); "Negro boy of light black complexion" with "long scr on the corner of right eye and one under the right jaw"
3. Born free in Isle of Wight County, on oath of Conney Brassey.
4. Norfolk, July 11, 1838
5. August 22, 1853

VINES, MIMA

1. Born circa 1795

2. Height: 5'4½"; "Free woman of rather light complexion" with "scar about a half inch from corner of left eye and parallel with it" [1835]; "Free negro woman of black complexion" with "scar about a half an inch from the corner of left eye and parallel with it" 1847]
3. Born free in Southampton County
4. Southampton County, December 21, 1835; Norfolk, July 19, 1847
5. September 24, 1838 and July 26, 1858

WALK, SOLOMON

1. Born circa 1801
2. Height: 5'11 and 3/8ths in shoes"; "Dark mulatto man, scar on right arm, between elbow and shoulder and mole on right side of face."
3. "Emancipated by will of Samuel Colton, dated August 26, 1837, recorded March 5, 1841"
4. Elizabeth City County, May 24, 1849
5. July 23, 1849

WALKER, CLARA ("CLARA, ALIAS CLARA WALKER")

1. Born 1826 or earlier
2. Height: 5'5½"; "Light complexion, long hair, scar on right cheek under eye"
3. Emancipated with father by will of William Allen, deceased, recorded February 23, 1832
4. Surry County, February 22, 1847
5. February 25, 1850

WALKER, ELEANORA
(Daughter of Polly Walker)

1. Born circa 1848
2. Height not taken [she was two]; "Bright mulatto complexion, straight hair, no mark or scar visible"
3. Born free in Norfolk, proved by oath of Elizabeth Donaldson
4. Norfolk, March 4, 1850
5. July 26, 1858

WALKER, POLLY

1. Born circa 1828

2. Height: 5'6¾"; "Free woman of mulatto complexion" with "small black mole on side of neck, near jawbone"
3. Born free in Norfolk, proved by oath of Elizabeth Donaldson
4. Norfolk, March 4, 1850
5. July 26, 1858
6. Living in Norfolk City on August 9, 1850, the U.S. Census reveals :

> Polly Walker, 23, female, white
> Walter Walker, 3, male, white
> Ellenora Walker, 5, female, white

On July 18, 1860, the family was enumerated by the census in Norfolk:

> Polly Walker, 30, female, mulatto, laundress
> Walt Walker, 15, male, mulatto, app. barber
> Ellen Walker 12, female, mulatto

When the census takers found the family in Norfolk on August 20, 1870, the children had changed their surnames:

> Bluford, Walter, 23, male, black, barber
> Walker, Polly, 39, female, mulatto, washes and irons
> Bluford, Elenora, 18, female, mulatto
> Goodson, Cathy, 60, female, mulatto, "works out"

None of them could read or write

On June 4, 1880, Walter Bluford was enumerated in Norfolk. He was 31, and a mulatto, and a "barbour"; his wife was Jane, age 25, also a mulatto, born in Virginia, and they had two children, Venus, 8, a girl, and Robert, 5.

WALKER, WALTER
(Son of Polly Walker)

1. Born circa 1845
2. Height not taken [he was five]; "Bright mulatto complexion, straight hair, mole on left arm, near elbow joint"
3. Born free in Norfolk, proved by oath of Elizabeth Donaldson
4. Norfolk, March 4, 1850
5. July 26, 1858
See Walker, Polly

WARREN, MARTHA

1. Born circa 1821
2. Height 5'½", "Woman of black complexion [with a] scar on right finger" [1842 and 1847]
3. Born free in Southampton County
4. Southampton County, October 20, 1842, and Norfolk, March 31, 1847 "having removed to this city to labor therein"
5. March 22, 1847 and July 27, 1858

WARRICK [or WARWICK], RICHARD

1. Born circa 1807
2. Height 5'7½", "Man of dark complexion with a scar on upper lip from a cut and the thumb of right hand scarred from being mashed" and in 1846 "face lightly pitted with the small pox."
3. Born free
4. Norfolk County, February 19, 1844; November 23, 1846
5. November 24, 1851

WARWICK, WILLIAM

1. Born circa 1809 [1836] or 1805 [1838]
2. Height: 5'10";"Bright mulatto" with "scar near corner of left eye and dark mole on palm of left hand" [1836] "Bright mulatto" with "scar on the nose near the corner of left eye and a dark mole in the palm of left hand" [1838]
3. Born free in Norfolk County and "removed from there to this Borough to reside therein"
4. Norfolk County, June 21, 1836; Norfolk, February 5, 1838
5. January 24, 1838 and October 25, 1853
6. William Warrick appears in the U.S. Census of 1860 in the Second Ward of Philadelphia along with his large family:

> William Warrick, 52, mulatto, steward; value of real estate: $1300; personal estate: $500
> Louisa Warrick, 59, mulatto
> William Warrick, 27, mulatto, barber
> Mary Warrick, 25, mulatto
> Mitchell Warrick, 20, mulatto, barber
> Lydia Warrick, 18, mulatto
> Bolton Warrick, 15, mulatto
> Charles Warrick, 13, mulatto

Louisa Warrick, 9, mulatto
Richard Warrick, 6, mulatto
All the Warricks were literate; all were born in Virginia, which means
that the family moved north between 1854 and 1860.

WATSON, ELIZABETH
(Formerly Rogers)

1. Born circa 1826
2. Height: 5'4½"; "Negro woman of bright mulatto complexion" with
"small scar on forehead over left eye, in edge of hair"
3. Born free in Norfolk, proven by oath of James Mitchell
4. Norfolk, November 1, 1850
5. July 26, 1858
6. "She is allowed to go at large until next Court, Wm W Lamb,
Mayor, July 21, 1858"

WATSON, MARY ANN
(Daughter of Elizabeth Watson)

1. Born circa 1846
2. Height: 3'3¼" [she was 4]; "Child of bright brown complexion"
with "no apparent mark or scar"
3. Born free in Norfolk, proven by oath of Rebecca Jones
4. Norfolk, November 1, 1850
5. July 26, 1858

WATKINS, PHOEBE (of)

1. Born circa 1808
2. Height: 5'4"; "Brown complexion, no apparent mark or scar."
3. Born free in Nansemond County, "having removed therefrom to
this city to labor therein"
4. Nansemond County, registry renewed September 11, 1843;
Norfolk, January 4, 1848
5. July 26, 1853

WATTS, BARTLEY

1. Born c. 1798
2. Height: 5'7"; "Black man with no apparent mark or scar on head, hands, or face,"
3. Emancipated by George Joliff by deed July 20, 1833
4. Norfolk, April 18, 1834; January 3, 1837
5. July 28, 1851

WATTS. FEREBEE

1. Born circa 1805
2. Height: 5'2½"; "Woman of light complexion" with "mark near right eye"
3. Born free in Norfolk County
4. Norfolk County, December 20, 1830; Norfolk, February 6, 1840
5. July 25, 1853

WATTS, MARGARET ANN
("Child of Ferebe Watts, free woman of color")

1. Born circa 1835
2. Height: 5'½"; "Negro girl of black complexion" with "mark on right side of nose"
3. Born free in Norfolk, proved by oath of Jonah Deans
4. Norfolk, March 12, 1850
5. August 25, 1856

WEBB, WILLIAM

1. Born circa 1811
2. Height 5'9", "Negro man of dark complexion [with] no apparent mark or scar"
3. Born free in Norfolk County
4. Norfolk County, February 19, 1844; Norfolk, November 23, 1846
5. November 23, 1846 and July 26, 1858

WEST, EMELINE

1. Born circa 1822
2. Height 5'2½, "Negro woman of dark complexion [with] scar on her jawbone under the left ear"
3. Born free in Isle of Wight County

4. Isle of Wight County, October 3, 1843
5. April 27, 1844

WEST, HARRIET

1. Born circa 1826
2. Height: 5'7½"; "Bright mulatto with small scar on wrist, occasioned by the cut of a knife"
3. Born free in Princess Anne County
4. Princess Anne County, December 6, 1847, "removed therefrom to this City to labor therein" and Norfolk, March 5, 1850
5. February 27, 1850 and June 28, 1858

WHITE, ACQUEY

1. Born circa 1779
2. Height: 5'4½'; "Negro man of black complexion" with "large scar on inside of right arm, below elbow and wrist"
3. Emancipated by Marshall Parks by deed, April 17, 1824, Norfolk
4. Norfolk, October 7, 1850
5. July 26, 1858
6. "Permission is granted, May 27, 1837, to remain in state"
"Ackey" White was enumerated by the Census in Norfolk City on August 13, 1850. His age was given as "70", his color as "black", his occupation as "drayman." He had $500 of real estate. His household included wife, Rachael, age 60, black; Margaret Cunningham, age 23, mulatto, Amy White, age 15, black, and George Bowser, age 10, black. Ackey and Rachael White and Margaret Cunningham were illiterate, but Amy White and George Bowser could read and write.

WHITE, AMY

1. Born circa 1835
2. Height not taken [1838]; 4'10" [1850]; "Negro child of light black complexion" with "scar under left ear and middle of neck, occasioned by a rising".
3. "Emancipated from Ackey White by deed bearing date of June 25, 1838, recorded June 25, 1838
4. Norfolk, October 2, 1838 and December 9, 1850
5. November 25, 1850 and July 26, 1858
6. "Daughter of Rachael White"; Amy White, age 15, appears with

her parents Ackey and Rachael in the U.S. Census of 1850 for Norfolk

WHITE, DANIEL
(Son of Sally White)

1. Born circa 1826
2. Height: 5'9½"; "Man of mulatto complexion" with "no apparent mark or scar"
3. Born free in Norfolk
4. Norfolk, September 6, 1849
5. July 28, 1858
6. The U.S. Census of 1880 shows that on June 4 of that year, Daniel S. White, "mulatto, male, age 56", was living at 173 Turner's Lane in the City of Norfolk, and working as a laborer. Living with him was his wife, Ann, "mulatto, female, age 40", who worked as a "washwoman." Neither Mr. nor Mrs. White could read or write.

WHITE, DAVID

1. Born circa 1781
2. Height: 5'9" ("in shoes"); "A man of dark complexion with a scar on his forehead in line with his nose and one in his right cheek below the eye, occasioned both by cuts; also a scar on his right hand near wrist and one on his right arm just above the wrist, the first occasioned by a burn and the second by a cut."
3. "Emancipated by the deed of Richard Walke, administrator of Isaac Talbot, dec., and husband of Mary Diane Talbot, the daughter of said Isaac, who is now Mary Diana Walke and Sarah W. Talbot, widow of said Isaac and guardian of Isaac Talbot, infant orphan of Isaac Talbot, dec.", March 1, 1838
4. Norfolk Borough, March 5, 1838
5. July 25, 1853
6. David White, age 70, appears in the U.S. Census of 1850 in Norfolk. He is described as "black" and illiterate. He was working as a ship's carpenter. Enumerated with him were, Jane, age 54, "black," and illiterate—evidently his wife, as well as an unmarried daughter, Berthenia, age 28, also "black," and illiterate, as well as two other daughters, Elizabeth, age 35, "black", and literate, and Sarah, 25, "black," and literate. There are four younger members of the household: Martha A., age 15, Eliza, age 11, George 7, and John 4, all "black", who would seem to be the children of Elizabeth. (Jane White,

one would suppose, would have been unlikely to have borne children at the ages of 47 and 51, and Berthenia and Sarah would seem to have perhaps been too young, age 28 and 25, to have a 15 year old child).

WHITE, DICK

"On the application of Dick White, a slave emancipated since the first day of May 1806, the acting justices of this city, having been summoned and a majority of them being present, and it appeared to the Court that notice of this application has been posted at the front door of the Courthouse of this city for at least two monks preceding this day, and the attorney for the Commonwealth appearing on behalf of the Commonwealth and defending this application—and it appearing to the satisfaction of the Court that the said Dick White is a person of good character, peaceable, orderly, and industrious, not addicted to drunkenness or gaming or any other vice—and three fourths of the justices present concurring herein permission is granted the said Dick White to remain within the Commonwealth and reside within the city only during the good pleasure of the Court, to which order Wm. D. Debney, Mayor, dissented. John Williams, January 28, 1861"

WHITE, EDWARD

1. Born circa 1805
2. Height: 5'9" ; [part of register is missing] "small scar on forehead"
3. Emancipated in Norfolk by deed by C.C. Taylor on October 27, 1851
4. Norfolk, February 18, 1852
5. July 26, 1858

WHITE, ELIZABETH
("Elizabeth White, formerly Elizabeth Oden")

1. Born circa 1831
2. Height: 5'1½"; "Negro woman of brown complexion" with "small scar on left hand at root of forefinger and another on left side of cheek, near ear"
3. Born free in Norfolk, proved by evidence of John S. Belote
4. Norfolk, November 30, 1850
5. July 26, 1858

WHITE, GRACE

1. Born circa 1815
2. Height" 5' 1¼"; "Free negro woman of light black complexion with small scar near right corner of mouth, two scars on the right arm, on the inner side of the elbow joints, having lost sight in the left eye."
3. Born free in Norfolk, proved by oath of John Shuster
4. Norfolk, May 28, 1838 and October 8, 1845
5. May 24, 1852

WHITE, MARTHA BERRY

1. Born circa 1818
2. Height: 5'4¾"; "A free woman of bright mulatto complexion with straight hair and full hazel eyes, no apparent mark or scar on head, face, or hands worthy of notice" [1842]; "Free woman of light mulatto complexion, straight hair and full hazel eyes, upper front teeth being decayed", "no apparent mark or scar on head, face, or hands" [1852]
3. Born free in York County
4. Norfolk Borough, September 25, 1842 and February 19, 1852
5. October27, 1851 and July 26, 1858
6. In the U.S. Census of 1850, Martha White, age 30, was enumerated with her husband Edmund, age 40, a "drayman" who owned property worth $500.00, and her children: Walter (5), Mary Eliza (4), and James (1). All were described as "mulatto." Neither Edmund nor Martha could read or write.

WHITE, MARY FRANCES

1. Born circa 1831
2. Height: 4'11"; "Negro woman of black complexion" with "scar on the nose, another on the chin, a small one on little finger of left hand"
3. Born free in Norfolk, proved by oath of Maria Roberts
4. Norfolk, July 27, 1850
5. Norfolk, July 27, 1858
6. Mary Frances White had a child, CORNELIUS GRAY, "a negro child of light brown complexion", age 16 months, who was also registered.

WHITE, RACHAEL

1. Born circa 1792
2. Height: 5'½"[in 1838]; 4'11" [in 1850]; "Negro woman of black complexion...has wen on inside of right arm near wrist" [1840]; "Negro woman of black complexion" with "no apparent mark or scar"
3. "Emancipated by deed from Ackey White, bearing date June 25, 1838
4. Norfolk, October 2, 1838 and December 9, 1850
5. November 25, 1850 and July 26, 1858
6. The U.S. Census on August 13, 1850 enumerated Rachael White in Norfolk City:

Ackey White, 70, male, black, Drayman, value of real estate $500

Rachael White, 60, female, black
Margaret Cunningham, 23, female, black
Amy White, 15, female, black
George Bowser, 10, male, black

The three adult members of the family could neither read nor write, but the two younger ones apparently could. It is interesting that Mrs. White's husband's name was identical to that of her master! Amy may have been their daughter. Since the census of 1850 did not record the relationship of the members of a household to the "head", it is impossible to determine whether Cunningham and Bowser were related. On August 9, 1860 the census-takers found the Whites again in the City of Norfolk:

Archy [sic] White, 84, male, black, no occupation stated, value of real estate $300
Rachel White, 70, female, black, no occupation stated
Amy White, age 25, female, black, no occupation stated

WHITE, SYLVIA
(Daughter of Sally White)

1. Born circa 1815
2. Height: 5'1½" [1837]; 5'1 and seven eighths" [1853]; "Woman of mulatto complexion"; "slightly pitted with the smallpox on the nose and forehead"

5. January 28, 1861
6. 'I am unable to ascertain whether or not she is the descendant of a female negro who was emancipated since the first of May 1806" [Clerk, 1853]

WILLIAMS, JAMES

1. Born circa 1821
2. Height: 5'6"; "Negro man of mulatto complexion" with "slight scar on middle joint of left thumb"
3. Born free in Southampton County
4. Norfolk, February 27, 1850
5. July 26, 1858
6. According to the U.S. Census of 1870, living in the city of Norfolk on August 18, were:

> Williams, James, age 50, mulatto, huckster, illiterate
> Williams, Lucy, age 45, black, keeps house
> Williams, Hannah 16, mulatto, attending school
> Williams, James 10, mulatto attending school
> Harris, Charley, age 22, mulatto, clerk in store
> Harris, Sarah, age 20, black, domestic servant
> Harris, Ellen, age 1, mulatto

The Census for the city of Norfolk in 1880 shows:

> Williams, James, mulatto, age 58, grocer-dealer, illiterate
> Williams, Lucy, black, age 60, keeping house, illiterate
> Williams, Annie, black, age, 28, dressmaker, literate
> Williams, James, black, age 21, clerk in store, literate
> Harris, Sarah, black, age 30, domestic servant, literate
> Harris, Eliza, black, age 11, At school
> Harris, Benjamin, black, age 3
> Wilson, Laura, black, age 23, Keeping house

The 1880 census, which gives relationships, indicates that Sarah Harris and Laura Wilson were James William's married daughters. Mrs. Harris' husband, Charley, must have died between 1877, when their son Benjamin was born, and 1880.

WILLIAMS, JOHN

1. Born circa 1819
2. Height: 5'2½"; "Man of black complexion" with "scar on the right temple on a line with outer corner of eye"

3. Born free in Norfolk, proved by oath of Thomas Hawkins
4. Norfolk, April 9, 1850
5. August 26, 1856

WILLIAMS, LUCINDA, see HOLLAND, LUCINDA

WILLIAMS, MATILDA JACKSON

1. Born circa 1834
2. Height" 4'9¾" [at 17]; "Dark complexion" with "two scars on left arm and very much scarred on the back"
3. Emancipated in Norfolk by James Murphy in deed dated January 24, 1843
4. Norfolk, May 29, 1851
5. July 26, 1858

WILLS, MARGARET

1. Born circa 1803
2. Height: 5'1"; "Free woman of mulatto complexion" with "no visible mark or scar on head, face, or hands"
3. Born free in Norfolk
4. Norfolk, October 7, 1845
5. July 26, 1858

WILLOUGHBY, NANCY COOK

1. Born circa 1787
2. Height: 5'1"; "Light complexion" with "circular scar on left jaw"
3. "Born free, as determined by a jury at March Court 1819 against Zenger Ivy
4. Norfolk County, September 21, 1835

5. April 23, 1835
See Cook, Polly

WILSON, ANTHONY

1. Born circa 1823
2. Height: 5'2¾"; "Black complexion; scar on bridge of nose and two black marks or scars on the inside of the right wrist"

3. Freed by will of Susan Clowes, deceased, recorded August 28, 1843
4. Norfolk Borough, April 28, 1845
5. June 28, 1858
6. See Wilson, Patience and Anthony

WILSON, BETSEY [Her register is crumbled and partially illegible]

1. Born circa 1813
2. Height: 5'1"; "Light complected", scar on forehead
3. [Illegible]
4. Princess Anne County, October [day illegible] 1831
5. July 31, 1858

WILSON, JOHN
(Son of Betsey Wilson)

1. Born circa 1835
2. Height: 4'9 and five eighths" [at 16]; "Negro boy of black complexion" with "small scar on forehead over left eye and several small scars on forefinger of left hand"
3. Born free in Norfolk, proven by oath of George Crow
4. Norfolk, May 12, 1851
5. July 26, 1858
6. "I am unable to state whether or not he is a descendant of a female slave emancipated since first day of May 1806"

[WILSON], LYDIA

1. Born circa 1824
2. Height: 5' and seventh eighths"; "scar on back of right wrist and small mole on right cheek and one near left corner of mouth"
3. Emancipated in Norfolk by last will and testament of Susan Clowes
4. Norfolk, September 2, 1853
5. April 23, 1860
6. Mrs. Wilson appears in Norfolk City in the Census of 1850, on July 9. Her age is given as 33, her color as "black", and her occupation as laundress. She was unable to read and write. Living with her was Rheuben Wilson, black, age 13, perhaps a son. On September 16, 1870, the census shows her living across the river in Portsmouth, Virginia. At the age of 43, working as a domestic servant, and

illiterate, she is the head of a household that included Cassy, black, age 10, and the twins Mary and Martha, age 4. She also appears in the Census of 1900, on June 1, in Norfolk's Fourth Ward. She was living then with a granddaughter, Lizzie Parnell, who was 25, and Lizzie's children, Lydia and Charles, age six and two, respectively. Lydia Wilson's month of birth is given as May, 1825.

WILSON, MARIA

1. Born circa 1829
2. Height: 5'; "Negro woman of light black complexion" with "scar on right cheek"
3. Emancipated in Norfolk by last will and testament of Susan Clowes, recorded August 20, 1843
4. Norfolk, June 7, 1852
5. July 26, 1858
6. See Wilson, Patience

WILSON, MARY

1. Born circa 1820
2. Height: 5'5½; "Mulatto woman of very bright complexion"; "no apparent mark or scar on head, hands, or face:
3. Born free in Norfolk Borough, proved by oath of Robert E. Taylor
4. Norfolk Borough, November 26, 1838
5. August 23, 1852

WILSON, MARY ANN

1. Born circa 1824
2. Height: 5'4½: "Mulatto woman with scar on her forehead"
3. Born free in Isle of Wight County
4. Isle of Wight County, May 2, 1846; Norfolk City, September 2, 1850
5. February 25, 1852

[WILSON], PATIENCE

1. Born circa 1830
2. Height: 4'9½"; "Free negro girl of light black complexion" with "three small moles on left shoulder"

3. Emancipated by last will and testament of Susan Clowes, deceased, August 28, 1843
4. Norfolk, February 26, 1850
5. July 26, 1858
6. The "register" of Patience has only her given name, but the index to the 1850 census provided by Ancestry.com shows only one woman of color in Norfolk City named "Patience", and her age corresponds exactly to that given in the register. In August, 1850, the following persons shared a household:

> Maria Wilson, 22, female, black
> Patience Wilson, 20, female, black
> Anthony Wilson, 25, male, black
> Reuben Wilson, 4, male, mulatto
> John Wilson 2 months, male, mulatto

No occupation is given for the three adults, none of whom could read or write.

On July 20, 1860, Patience Wilson, 30, female, mulatto, was enumerated by the census in Norfolk City, as the servant of a 22 year old white female named "S. Randolph."

WILSON, PETER

1. Born circa 1826
2. Height: 5'7½"; "Dark complexion, scar near ball of his thumb on right hand and several on back of right and left hands."
3. Born free in Isle of Wight County
4. Isle of Wight County, September 4, 1847
5. June 17, 1848

WILSON, WILLIAM

1. Born circa 1808
2. Height: 5'4½"; "A mulatto man" with "small scar on forefinger of left hand, a little above knuckle"
3. "Born of a free woman" in Isle of Wight County
4. Norfolk, September 3, 1835
5. July 25, 1853

WITFIELD, CREASY

1. Born circa 1824
2. Height 5'4", "A woman of yellow complexion...with a scar on left hand and one on lower lip"
3. Born free in Southampton County
4. Southampton County, October 19, 1844
5. October 21, 1844

WRIGHT, HARRIET
(Daughter of Hester Wright)

1. Born circa 1825
2. Height: 5'5"; "Free negro woman of black complexion; scar on the inner side of left arm at elbow joint"
3. Born free as proved by oath of William Jarvis
4. Norfolk, December 30, 1846 and August 15, 1853
5. July 26, 1853 and January 28, 1861
6. "Renewal of register at next term of Corporation Court", Wm. W. Lamb, Mayor, January 17, 1861"

WRIGHT, HESTER (of)

1. Born circa 1784
2. Height: 5'6½"; "A free negro woman of black complexion" with "two scars on the left arm between the wrist and elbow"
3. Born free in Nansemond County
4. Norfolk, October 3, 1835, November 30, 1846, and August 15, 1853
5. July 25, 1853 and September 27, 1858
6. Hester Wright and her family were enumerated by the U.S. Census August 17, 1860 in Norfolk:

      Hester Wright, 64, female, black
      Nancy Wright, 28, female, black
      William H. Wright, 19, male, black
      Hester H. Wright, 18, female, black

No occupation is given for any of them. All of them could read and write.

WRIGHT, MARY ELIZA

1. Born circa 1829

against the peace and dignity of the Commonwealth of Virginia. On a presentment made by a Grand Jury upon the evidence of John Dyson a witness sworn and sent by the Court to the Grand Jury.

James Nimmo, Attorney for the Commonwealth

The Commonwealth of Virginia, To the Sergeant of Norfolk Borough, Greeting: You are hereby commanded t summon Beverly West, a free man of colour to appear before the Justices of our Hustings Court of Norfolk Borough, at the Court House of our said Borough, on the fourth Monday in March next to shew cause if any why he can why an information should not be filed against him on a presentment f the Grand Jury made against him for remaining in the State of Virginia more than twelve months after the date of his emancipation by James Mitchell since the 1st day of May 1806, to wit by deed dated March 1816—contrary to the act of the General Assembly in such case made and provided.

And have then there this writ, Witness John Williams, Clerk of our said Court at the Court House, the 21st day of December 1831—in the 56th year of the Commonwealth.

John Williams

1832
Mar: Rule to shew cause made absolute
1833
Dec 2d: Nolle Prosequi

All of this cases ended in "Nolle prosequi", which is defined as "a declaration that the plaintiff in a civil case or the prosecutor in a criminal case will drop prosecution of all or part of a suit or indictment."

In other words, in every instance, after about a year, the case was dropped against all the defendants.

It is not clear whether any or all of these thirteen persons were forced to leave the state. None of them seem to appear—anywhere—in the U.S. Census of 1850.

ANTHONY, PETER

Freed by Bernard Magnien, late of Norfolk County, by last will and testament proved November 15, 1819
Living in Elizabeth River Parish, Norfolk [Borough], in 1831

ASH, PHILLIS

Slave of Stephen Decatur, late of Borough of Norfolk, by deed May 28, 1822
Lived in Elizabeth River Parish in 1831

BOWDOIN, KIZZY

Freed by deed of John Boucher, resident of Borough of Norfolk, March 26, 1827
Living in Elizabeth River Parish, Norfolk [Borough] in 1831

BOWDOIN, NANCY

Freed by John Bowdoin, deceased, formerly a resident of Borough of Norfolk, subsequently of Surry County, by deed May 26, 1818
Living in Elizabeth River Parish in 1831

COLLINS, RACHAEL

Freed April 23, 1816 by Anne Steed (later Anne Camp)
Living in Elizabeth River Parish, Norfolk [Borough] in 1831

COOLEY, ALFRED

Freed by deed of Drayton M. Curtis, formerly of Borough of Norfolk, June 5, 1816
Living in Elizabeth River Parish, Norfolk [Borough] in 1831

COOLEY, LUCY

Freed by Drayton M. Curtis, June 5, 1816
Living in Elizabeth River Parish, Norfolk [Borough], 1831

JONAS, CYRUS

Freed by deed of Alexander Jordan of Norfolk, July 2, 1824

Living in Elizabeth River Parish, Norfolk [Borough], in 1831

PUGH, JENNY

Freed by deed by John Morgan, March 6, 1812
Living in Elizabeth River Parish, Norfolk [Borough], 1831

RANDALL, EDMUND

Freed by Amey Randall, a free woman of color, April 2, 1828
Living in Elizabeth River Parish, Norfolk [Borough], in 1831

REYNOLDS, MARY ANN

Freed by deed of Rose Reynolds, March 30, 1822
Living in Elizabeth River Parish, Norfolk [Borough], 1831

WEST, BEVERLY

Freed by deed of James Mitchell, April 6, 1816
Living in Elizabeth River Parish, Norfolk [Borough] in 1831

WILLIAMS, HANNAH

Freed by deed of Alexander Jordan of Norfolk, recorded January 27, 1833
Living in Elizabeth River Parish, Norfolk [Borough] in 1831

www.ingramcontent.com/pod-product-compliance
Lightning Source LLC
Chambersburg PA
CBHW070917270326
41927CB00011B/2609